Grace & Guts
What it takes to forgive.

Barbara Francis

Also by Barbara Francis

Unexpected Turns: Leaning into the Losses of Life
(Expert Publishing, Inc., 2007)

Following Him When I Can't See the End of the Road
(NewLife Publications, 2002)

An Invitation to Eavesdrop: Finding Yourself in the Psalms
(Bible study guide)

Private Conversations: Reflections on the Prayer Life of Jesus
(Bible study guide)

A Personal Study Guide for Following Him When I Can't See the End of the Road (Bible study guide)

ISBN 10: 1-931945-69-1
ISBN 13: 978-1-931945-69-1

Library of Congress Catalog Number: 2009927668

Printed in the United States of America

First Printing: June 2009

13 12 11 10 09   5 4 3 2 1

Expert Publishing, Inc.
14314 Thrush Street NW
Andover, MN 55304-3330
1-877-755-4966
www.expertpublishinginc.com

Contents

A Word of Thanks

There is a little scene in Deuteronomy 26 that is a touching portrayal of a thankful life. The assignment given to the children of Israel by God was a simple one: take the best of their crops, put it in their baskets, bring it to the temple of the Lord, and bow down. God then said, "Rejoice in all the good things the Lord God has given to you and your household."

I write about the good things the Lord has done for me, the ways he has changed my life, and how he is continuing to do so by his love and grace. I put the fruit from his work in my books, bring it to the Lord, and bow down in thanksgiving for his gifts to me. In this project I write about the ways he has helped me forgive myself and others. It has been the finest of gifts.

But as with any great venture, many people have lent a helping hand along the way. These people are in my basket, too. I am thankful for each one of you and the impact you've had on my life:

My husband, partner, and best friend for 35 years, Bob. Your love and commitment to me have reset the course of my life.

Bill, who has filled his basket with his bounties so this book could get life and lift.

Jeff, whose craftsmanship in editing humbles me.

Mike and your team, who have shown great kindness, generosity, and expertise with design and layout.

Harry and Sharron, whose wise counsel and keen planning have once again played a crucial role in making the book a reality.

Andrea, my friend for well over two decades who has partnered with me on everything I have written. You have invested untold hours helping me with books, Bible studies, and life. Whether we're playing on another continent, walking on the beach, or reading a manuscript, you've believed in me and encouraged me every step of the way. My life is better because you are my friend. To you I dedicate this book.

Introduction

Grace & Guts is about a topic I have gone to terrific lengths to avoid.

This book is not for those ultra-pious Christians who declare that of course we must forgive those who've hurt us because that's what we're called to do, period, so do it already.

It's not for those who don't, or won't, acknowledge the struggles inherent in being human, even a person who, with all her or his heart, aches to do what is right.

It's not for anyone who is unwilling to admit that there are moments in life, even seasons in life, long ones, when feelings and thoughts of vengeance, anger, enmity, bitterness, or resentment have their way with us—even for those of us who strive to follow the most elegant and extravagant forgiver of all time, Jesus.

No, for me, the issue of forgiveness is sorely personal.

It is the source of a profound degree of pain, anguish, struggle, and failure in my life.

That is why I have been so apprehensive for so long about writing a book on the subject of forgiveness.

Although forgiveness is the thickest of the threads that make up the cords of my Christian faith, I have wondered how I could possibly begin to talk to others about embracing, extending, and personalizing forgiveness when I still deal with bouts of revenge and retaliation myself.

I have known the bitter taste of unforgiveness for as long as I can remember.

I am not proud of this confession, but I've learned that acknowledging what is true is where transformation begins.

So, *Grace & Guts* is for those who admit they wrestle with unforgiveness on a daily (hourly? minute-by-minute?) basis.

It is for those of us who have been wounded for decades, and for others of us for whom the gash came just this morning.

It is for those of us who have been left bleeding, embittered, and in desperate need of liberation from the prison that unforgiveness inevitably erects around our hearts and souls.

It is for those honest freedom-yearners who wish there were a way to lighten the ever-present weight of their negative emotions, or a mystical blade that could somehow carve the difficult memories out of our lives.

It is for those courageous enough to understand that you and I will never make genuine progress by pretending that what happened didn't happen, or by clinging to some hope that the pain will go away if we ignore it long enough.

It is for those who are ready to face head-on and with brutal honesty the issue of unforgiveness and the wearisome emotions of regret, hatred, and self-loathing that go with it—and the tragic damage it can cause to those we hold most dear, to those we pray were closer to us, and, most pivotal of all, to ourselves.

In the brilliant, if hard-to-watch, film *Magnolia*, tycoon Earl Partridge realizes these very truths, but it is a revelation that comes too late. Dying in a hospital bed, he replays his life—how he was unfaithful to his first wife and abandoned her and their son, Frank. In the

> ## "I'll tell you the greatest regret of my life: I let my love go."

flashback, Frank, still a boy, has to care for his mother as she dies from cancer. Much later, Earl receives a death sentence from the very same disease; but he and Frank are estranged, and it becomes torturously evident how deeply Frank holds his father in contempt. Earl concludes, "I'll tell you the greatest regret of my life: I let my love go."

Just as in real life, Frank and Earl are hardly alone. *Magnolia* is filled with people who are dealing with issues of forgiveness and regret and, in particular, how the wounds of childhood play out in grown-up lives. One of the characters, a well-meaning policeman, Jim Kurring, muses, "The law is the law, and heck if I'm gonna break it. But if you can forgive someone...well, that's the tough part."

Nearly every character contends with the ramifications of wounds and unforgiveness, and as the film winds down, there is an incredible scene where frogs rain down from the heavens. What immediately leaps to mind is a passage in Exodus 8: "If you refuse to let them go, I will plague your whole country with frogs." Letting go, releasing, absolving, forgiving—it's as difficult an issue as there is in life, and the part many of us grapple with most is *how*.

Not long ago, a Gallup poll indicated that 94 percent of Americans believe forgiveness is a substantive issue in their lives, and 85 percent say they need help with how to go about it. How can we forgive injustices committed against us? How can we forgive people who have wronged us and wounded us? There is a part of me that doesn't believe they should get away with it. There is a part of me that wants them to pay for what they have done. And if I am honest—and I promise you I am going to be—I must call this for what it is. There is something inside me that wishes for retribution and even revenge.

In some corner of my heart, the idea of forgiving rather than getting even is all too foreign.

Yet, deep within, I also know unforgiveness is a poison to the soul that gradually and surreptitiously drains me of the abundance I could have in life.

The words of John of the Ladder, the seventh-century monk who for 40 years lived a solitary life at Mount Sinai, give me hope to press on: "If some are still dominated by their former bad habits, and yet can teach by mere words, let them teach.... For perhaps, being put to shame by their own words, they will eventually begin to practice what they teach."[1]

There is another side to the forgiveness Rubik's Cube, too.

It is the reality that I, also, have betrayed, abused, lied, or otherwise inflicted pain and suffering on friends, family, and others. The sting of such memories can drive people to despair, depression, perpetual dispiritedness, and, in some instances, even thoughts of whether life is worth continuing. "How could I have been so foolish?" "What was I thinking?" "Why do I hurt someone I love over and over again?" "How is it that I can so easily fall into the trap of taking love for granted?"

I know firsthand that running on this treadmill of not forgiving myself is no way to live. A person can miss out on so much.

I have a list of regrets that would be jarring to almost anyone, and maybe you do, too. If only our regrets could atone for the pain of our reality.

How on God's earth can *we* be forgiven?

That is an issue any book on forgiveness must address, and, in my experience, going there requires the two qualities for which *Grace & Guts* is named.

Forgiveness is so personal, so varied, and so complex. The scenarios are endless. Some struggle with forgiving themselves for a tragic *mistake* made years ago that led to heartbreaking consequences. Others, for the *innocent accident* that triggered a catastrophic result.

Whatever your circumstances may be, I believe *Grace & Guts* offers foundational principles on forgiveness that may be helpful to you.

I wrote *Grace & Guts* in the aftermath of a trio of back-to-back, devastating events in my life: the loss of a dear friend in an airplane crash, the death of my mother-in-law, and a numbing discovery, after 54 years, of some facts about my birth. The journey I will share with you has helped me immensely, although I am very much a stumbling, staggering work in progress when it comes to the elusive topic of forgiveness. This is a process, after all.

This much I can say with absolute certainty: God wants us to be free to *embrace* his forgiveness right at the spot most needed within us and to be free to *extend* forgiveness where it is most needed by others within the sphere of our lives. Dr. Lewis Smedes gets it right when he says, "Forgiveness is God's invention for coming to terms with a world in which, despite their best intentions, people are unfair to each other and hurt each other deeply. He began by forgiving us. And he invites us all to forgive each other."[2]

As we shall see, Jesus hung out with all kinds of people who were wronged by others and who managed, themselves, to wrong many in their lives. It was exceedingly high on Jesus' list to forgive them and to teach them how to forgive others. Why? Because forgiveness can be one of the most powerful forces for good in our own lives and in our world at large.

> **"Forgiveness is God's invention for coming to terms with a world in which, despite their best intentions, people hurt each other deeply."**

If you are tired of living with hurt, anger, regrets, or haunting memories, and you are fearful of becoming someone who is hard-hearted, harsh, unkind, or bitter, please know you are not alone and that *Grace & Guts* is written just for you.

While bravery will be required and everyone's journey is different, I believe you may find that forgiveness is not just a lofty, utopian ideal, but an attainable reality.

Here is a prayer that has helped me, and it may be worthwhile for you to consider it as we open this book together:

> *Lord, I so wish to prepare well for this time. I so want to make all of me ready and attentive and available to you.*
>
> *Please help me to clarify and purify my intentions. I have so many contradictory desires.*

I get preoccupied with things that don't really matter or last. I know that if I give you my heart, whatever I do will follow my new heart.

In all that I am today, all that I try to do, all my encounters, reflections, even frustrations and failings, and especially in this time of prayer—in all of this may I place my life in your hands.

Lord, I am yours. Make me what you will.

Amen.

—St. Ignatius of Loyola (1491-1556)[3]

The First Journey: Embracing Forgiveness

Can I Be Forgiven?

Forgiveness is the answer to the child's dream of a miracle by which what is broken is made whole again, what is soiled is again made clean.[4]

—Dag Hammarskjold
Winner of the Nobel Peace Prize

It's Not Just a Dream

She was four days old when her mother decided she had little choice but to give her up. She was placed in the home of a well-respected couple who lived in an affluent area with lush, tree-lined streets. She attended private schools and enjoyed many of the niceties of an upper-middle-class lifestyle. But like the Western town front in the back lot of a Hollywood production company, it was for the most part a façade. All was not well—so much so that as the years gathered, she couldn't help but wonder exactly what had happened in the earliest moments of her life to bring her into the anguished one she now lived.

She began to struggle intensely with issues of rejection and abandonment, a corrosive dynamic that accelerated in her adolescence—not just because she was adopted, but because of the many injustices she lived with on a daily basis. Whether in the school yard, her back yard, or under her own roof, it was a rare day that cruel practices did not leave her in tears.

Just below the surface of a seemingly put-together exterior, a deep anger and profound disappointment began to take hold. And with that anger and disappointment came reckless, self-destructive behaviors, one after the other. By her late teens, she could understand the worst sorts of pain and sorrow a young girl could inflict on herself or encounter in life. Without ever understanding exactly what drove her, she had accumulated a sordid history. Only when she heard the gospel of Jesus as a freshman in college did the long, complicated road to understanding, inner healing, and forgiveness begin. And even then, it was only a start.

For those who may be wondering about the fate of this young girl, I can tell you that she has come a long way, but she is still very much a work in progress. I know this because, if you haven't already guessed, I am that girl.

So much of my journey towards forgiveness begins with a moment in my life that unfolded when I was just four days old.

Growing up, I don't know that I ever sifted through much of the emotion I had deep inside me about my adoption. As a child, I didn't in any way want to hurt my adoptive mother, who tried so hard to soften the harshness in our home, by asking her questions about my birth mother. But by my teenage years, all the stuffed emotions merged with my general unhappiness, and I started acting out in ways that I would later come to deeply regret. And when, in later years, I began to delve into the significant issues of forgiveness in my life over a period of thirty-some years of trying to live the Christian life as best I could, I realized that the first place I needed to begin was maybe the toughest: myself.

I so understand what counselor, professor, and seminarian Vernon Grounds is getting at when he writes, "When for whatever reasons your personal world goes to pieces, is it possible to do more than simply manage to survive? If the whole structure of your existence is shattered, like a precious vase dropped on a hardwood floor, can those shards be gathered up and by some re-creative miracle be put together again into an object of beauty or usefulness?"[5]

My lengthy passage to forgiveness, and especially self-forgiveness, originated in the foggy aftermath of the sudden death some years ago of one of my dearest friends. I wrote about her death in *Unexpected Turns*, but it was a season of loss and of jarring change in my life, not only in my relationships, but also in my work. While, thankfully, I was blessed with a strong marriage and two healthy older kids, much of what had occupied my life suddenly was gone.

It took nearly two years to come to terms with my friend's death. But even after I had grieved her loss and made peace with what had happened, what had boiled up inside me were unresolved issues of rejection and abandonment and forgiveness.

I have come to understand that these issues are not unusual for adoptees, but it became obvious that my inner world needed serious attention.

My life was blessed on so many fronts, and yet I recognized that if I didn't unpack why I reacted with so much anger, bitterness,

> "When your world goes to pieces, is it possible to do more than simply manage to survive?"

and unforgiveness whenever I felt rejection or abandonment, I was in danger of becoming a very different person. It was going to change me. Bitterness, anger, self-centeredness, defensiveness, and a life-stealing self-guardedness threatened to turn me into something I did not want to become.

I spent hours on my back porch praying through the years of my life. I had to re-embrace a forgiveness of myself—even though, as a person who had decided to follow Jesus while in college years earlier, I knew I had already been given the gift of forgiveness by God.

I came to the Christian faith stumbling all the way. I knew so little about God. When I heard the gospel of Jesus and his not-of-this-world love, I knew at once I had a chance to turn over a new leaf in my life.

I didn't harbor grand expectations about the Christian life. It just presented a whole new way of living, and that is what I so badly needed.

More than anything else, it was the notion of being forgiven, the thought that I could place my head on the pillow each night and not be wracked with guilt or shame, that was so attractive to me and so healing.

As I prayed back through my life, as I reflected back on my prodigal teenage years, and as I stretched even further back to how my adoption might have impacted my inner life, I found freedom and tranquility in inviting Jesus into the darkest parts.

When I've done that in my life, there is something of the miraculous to it. It is hard to put into words.

Richard Foster, the theologian and author, says something similar about prayer. He observes that when he is writing about prayer, he is writing about something that lies beyond what his experience and his words can adequately describe.

For me, there was, and there is, something that happens with forgiveness when we invite God into the darkest places of our lives.

I believe God yearns for us to know we are fully wanted, fully loved, fully accepted. I also appreciate that it can take a lifetime to fully understand this truth.

John Newton, the 18th century slave-ship captain who eventually renounced the inhumanity he perpetrated on thousands of Africans, finally arrived at a profound comprehension of God's forgiveness and self-forgiveness. In the film that was inspired by his life and the brave life of British slavery abolitionist William Wilberforce, Newton observes, "God sometimes does His work with gentle drizzle, not storms. Drip. Drip. Drip."

"Two things I know. I am a great sinner and Christ is a great Savior."

The film is named for the ultra-famous song that Newton wrote, "Amazing Grace," and it captures Newton's incredible inner journey towards embracing forgiveness. "I wish I could remember all their names," Newton says. "My 20,000 ghosts, they all had names, beautiful African names." He goes on: "Though I have lost my memory, two things I know. I am a great sinner and Christ is a great Savior."

A close friend of mine, Diane, recently arrived at a similar place—realizing that she is both forgivable and forgiven—and, for reasons you will see, her voyage also required immeasurable quantities of courage and character.

It's not an exaggeration to say that Diane's story is almost every woman's worst nightmare.

She had a religious upbringing, and, as a young girl, she set her sights on becoming a nun once she graduated from high school. When she turned 18, however, she opted instead to attend college and pursue a nursing degree, soothing a deep-seated guilt over abandoning her promise with the thought that God would still be pleased with her so long as she dedicated ample time to working at her church, which she was pleased to do.

Flash forward a few years. She had a good job at a local hospital; she had two young children and a husband. Life had its ups and downs, but things were good overall.

But then one day, life began to slowly unravel.

Quite suddenly, her husband asked for a divorce, leaving her as a single mother of a one-year-old and a five-year-old. Privately, she began to wonder if what had happened to her marriage and family were because God had somehow given her a "black mark."

Her life was filled with meeting the demands of single parenthood and work, but she poured herself into volunteering even more fervently at church to try to "win back" God's approval. Then, to make financial ends meet, she took on extra work as an on-call nurse for surgical patients. Here is Diane's description of what happened next:

> *Late one night—thankfully a night when my children were with relatives—I returned home from an on-call appointment and encountered an intruder in my house. I became the victim of a violent crime. After beating and raping me, the criminal left me in bad shape, but I was able to call for help. The ambulance brought me to the very hospital where I worked.*

In and of itself, this would have demanded a long, complex road to recovery, but Diane also faced the daunting task of needing to support her family. She fought constant exhaustion and weakness.

Emotionally, I was far from healed. The one consolation I felt was the certainty that at least I could not become pregnant from the rape, as I had had a tubal ligation a year earlier. But even with that assurance, the next several weeks were desolate with depression and punctuated by anguished, raw moments. My daughter would often find me crying uncontrollably. But I had to keep going; there was simply no time to heal physically or emotionally from the attack and its devastating ramifications. It was the darkest place of my life: divorced, a single mom, and now an exhausted, despondent rape victim.

Two months after the attack, she began feeling ill, and a doctor's visit confirmed the inconceivable reality that she had become pregnant as a result of the rape. Her doctor explained to her that there is still a miniscule chance of conception after a tubal ligation—one in 8,000—and, unfortunately, she was the one.

> "I became the victim of a violent crime. After beating and raping me, the criminal left me in bad shape."

Barely holding her family together as it was, she faced relentless internal conflict, and her closest counselor and friend, the medical director of the hospital where she worked, strongly recommended she terminate her pregnancy. More than anything else, Diane felt utterly alone.

Coming from a stringent religious background, I struggled to even consider abortion as a viable option. On one hand, I figured, if I had this child, God just might finally accept me, love me, and grant me the golden ticket into heaven. I had worked my whole life trying to please him and win his favor. Keeping this child would surely prove I was serious in my devotion. On the other hand, I had the notion that God would condemn me for all eternity if I terminated my pregnancy, committing one of the most terrible sins I'd ever been warned about.

Feeling that her life was steadily spinning out of control and struggling to hold her family together as it was, let alone adding a newborn baby into the equation, she made the anguishing decision to follow the counsel of her friend and medical director, and she got the abortion.

The darkness that had plagued my soul for weeks blackened even more. I was quite sure any opportunity to know God and be with him for all eternity was forever gone. I knew with certainty there was no hope for forgiveness for someone like me who aborted her own child. I was doomed and I had no one to blame but myself. I could not forgive myself for what I had done.

The weight of what she had done was never far from her mind, but the next few years brought flashes of hope. For her children's sake, she relocated her family to North Carolina to be close to her parents. She busied herself endlessly with a new job, her children, and volunteer work at her church. Then she met a man whom she would eventually marry, and she befriended a woman who invited her to a Bible study. At the very first study session, Diane heard a story that seemed to be exactly what she needed to hear. It introduced her to the Old Testament prophet Elijah, who had worked tirelessly on God's behalf, and yet Elijah despaired that he had somehow let God down. This captured precisely how Diane had felt for many years.

In subsequent conversations with a friend and a minister, Diane slowly came to the realization that God's favor for her could not be

> "God's favor for her could not be **revoked because of anything she** had done ... his inexplicable grace **through Jesus was a gift.**"

revoked because of anything she had done, that his inexplicable grace through Jesus was a gift. Her task—and it was not an easy one in her case—was simply to accept this lavish love of God.

In time, in Diane's own words, "I began to feel free for the first time in my life."

Diane's journey towards fully embracing that she is forgivable and forgiven continues. From time to time, she has been plagued with the thought that telling her story will make her an outcast. That is not an uncommon worry for those of us reaching for forgiveness and who have much for which we need to be forgiven. At times I have seen that some of us keep quiet about aspects of our lives we are ashamed of because we suspect that love will be withdrawn or withheld altogether. When we give in to such a fear, even if it's a reasonable one and may in fact be realized in some instances, we can miss out on experiencing forgiveness at the deepest levels. In Diane's case, letting it out has led to her being surrounded by a community of loving friends.

Embracing forgiveness is not tidy. It is messy. It is a gamble. But it is one worth taking.

In Matthew 4:23-25 of *The Message*, a contemporary paraphrase of the Bible by pastor, scholar, author, and poet Eugene Peterson, Jesus is described as healing people from the "bad effects of their bad lives." Who did this include and who came to see him? "Anybody with an ailment," Peterson writes, "whether mental, emotional, or physical. Jesus healed them, one and all."

After a lifetime of thinking she was unhealable and unforgivable, Diane has discovered that both are very much within her grasp. Her story is not easy to tell or hear, and yet, how thankful I am for people like Diane who are willing to tell their painful but beautiful stories in order to help others along the difficult journey toward

> "Embracing forgiveness is not tidy. It is messy. It is a gamble. But it's one worth taking."

receiving forgiveness. With grace and guts, Diane has provided us a glimpse of what it can look like to transform a difficult past into a beautiful present, even in her own eyes.

Given my past, I have had many quiet nights to ponder the questions, *Why is it so tough for some of us to forgive ourselves?* and *Why is it that we feel we must continue to punish ourselves?*

At least for me, there exists within me a part that feels so right not to forgive myself when I have really screwed up. *What is that about?* I have wondered.

Perhaps part of the answer can be traced back to my inability to escape the memory of what I said or didn't say, what I did or didn't do. Maybe this is something you can relate to. The truth is, when I have done or said something I later regretted, I am haunted by the fact that it did not have to happen, and I am compelled to ask myself what it is within me that made me choose the course of action I took. I struggle to get away from the mental reminders associated with my mistake, and there seems to be no way of eluding them.

Singer-songwriter Mason Jennings evokes the inner strife of forgiving oneself in his song, "Forgiveness":

> *Sitting on a bench in an old time station*
> *Waiting for a train to forgiveness*
> *I've brought no baggage, I've come here alone*
> *Looking for a way to forgiveness…*
> *All these broken pieces of arrows in my side*
> *I thought I could run with them, I know now I can't hide,*
> *So I'm looking out upon the darkness down the tracks*
> *Looking for the light of forgiveness…*[6]

I cannot help but nod in knowing understanding when, in the film *The Fisher King*, a doctor tells a radio deejay who is desperately seeking forgiveness in the aftermath of a terrible tragedy, "The brain never loses anything—it just stores it up and waits. A person could actually re-experience the full effect of a tragedy long after the event took place."

Another reason some people find it is so hard to forgive themselves is that we are prone to devising unrealistic expectations for ourselves. Or, in other cases, some of us are prisoners of perfectionism, and we fail to allow for the frailties of our humanity. Thus, when we fall short of an arbitrary ideal, we can end up broken and bent.

Then there are those foolish assumptions like: "I would never do that" or "I am strong enough to withstand whatever temptation comes my way." But the truth is, even on our best days, all of us *are* capable of wrongdoing and causing hurt or suffering, willful or otherwise.

Another significant component as to why we are pained to forgive ourselves—and perhaps the toughest to overcome—is the tragic fact that so many of us believe we *deserve* to be punished. We *deserve* to suffer. For many of us, there resides a still, small voice in our heads that ceaselessly reminds us with painfully terse *told-you-so*'s.

Forgiving oneself is not for cowards.

In nearly every instance, the events that create the need for us to forgive ourselves are moments in time we would wish away in a heartbeat if we had the power.

Instead, we are compelled to dwell on the hard reality that it is so difficult to live a life marked by virtuous, loving decisions, even for those of us trying to live out our Christian faith.

Novelist Annie Dillard, who traverses the unsparing terrain of forgiveness and reconciliation in her novel *The Maytrees*, in which a man who was unfaithful to his wife finds himself seeking an agonizing favor from her 20 years later, puts it so well: "There is no shortage of good days. It is good lives that are hard to come by."[7]

So, *can* we be forgiven? Where do we go from here? For those of us struggling with such issues, how do we get past the pain of our mistakes, the shame, the self-condemnation, the regret for the damage we've caused? Can our broken lives, like the vase in Vernon Grounds' earlier statement, be put together again?

Yes.

No matter what it is we have done, so long as we are willing to work hard, so long as we are able to give it some time, the answer is yes.

The path to embracing and receiving forgiveness involves numerous steps—at least that describes what has worked for me. First, we need to be willing to face facts and acknowledge what has happened. One more day of denial gets us nowhere. Painful as it is, honesty is essential. Second, I have learned the hard way I cannot attain forgiveness if I am blaming someone else for whatever transpired. Brutal honesty here, too, is required. Third, our hope for a redemptive miracle rests in our willingness to embrace God's unconditional love and forgiveness, evidenced by the sending of his son, Jesus Christ, to take all the weight of our sin on himself. *This* is so paramount to receiving forgiveness. This was Diane's story. And it is mine. The light bulb went on for both of us when we understood who Jesus is and what he has done for us.

Musician and global social activist Bono touches on this very insight—the relationship between God and forgiving oneself—when he describes in a *New York Times* article how he views Easter: "It's a transcendent moment for me—a rebirth I always seem to need. Never more so than a few years ago, when my father died. I recall the embarrassment and relief of hot tears as I knelt in a chapel in a village in France and repented my prodigal nature—repented for fighting my father for so many years and wasting so many opportunities to know him better. I remember the feeling of 'a peace that passes understanding' as a load lifted."[8]

Because of grace, I know that feeling, the "peace" that lifts years of burden. But I also know that when we have lived with years of guilt, regret, and shame connected to past actions, we often can become convinced we don't merit forgiveness. Being forgiven seems impossible, unattainable. So when we hear it is possible, something in us has a tendency to reject it out of hand. I rejected it for far too long.

After years of attempts and efforts, I have gradually learned a process that has helped me receive and embrace God's forgiveness. It is a three-pronged approach to the "how" of forgiving myself, and it has become a sort of spiritual discipline in my life for some time now:

Own It Deeply

It is human nature to struggle with owning our mistakes. Often, we resort to blame-shifting, finger-pointing, side-stepping, and justifying our actions. Or some of us prefer to wallow in an ocean of self-pity and bottomless regret that keeps us locked in a vicious cycle of unforgiveness. I did both for far too long. Dr. Phil, psychologist and popular television talk show host, often asks, "How's it working for you?" My own response, when it comes to the blaming and wallowing approach? Lousy. Blaming others or beating ourselves up will never give us the release we so desperately need in order to experience forgiveness. Heartfelt admission of our responsibility is the first key that unlocks the door to personal freedom.

But we need to keep in mind another facet of forgiveness. I mentioned this caveat in the introductory comments: Some deep regrets and jagged wounds are linked to an action that was truly an accident, a split-second of inattention that can visit a terrible tragedy on a stranger or a friend or a family member. The entire premise of the film *The Garden State* is the impact on a father and son when the son, at the age of nine, pushes his mother in a moment of childish anger, and she is paralyzed as a result.

Even in such instances, when what happened was categorically unintended but has caused years of nightmares, pain, *what-if*s, and guilt, it remains crucial to be honest and own the facts of the event. As grueling as that may be, it is a necessary step on the path to forgiveness.

> "Blaming ourselves or beating ourselves up will never give us the release we so desperately need in order to experience forgiveness."

From a biblical perspective, forgiveness is based on the finished work of Jesus on the cross. His death on the cross provides forgiveness for both the accidental mistakes we make and for the deliberate sins we commit. God's plan is disrupted by both; Jesus' sacrifice atones completely for both. I love what 1 John 1:9 says: "If we confess our sins, he is faithful and just to forgive us our sins and purify us from all unrighteousness." What is our part? To confess our sins.

Confession consists of simply agreeing with God about our wrong choices. Emotionally, we are broken and deeply sorrowful that we have hurt the God who loves us, either directly or by hurting others. We then turn away from the very acts that nailed Jesus to the cross. This is called repentance. God then does his part, to forgive and purify us. But if we are being honest, confession—truly owning our wrong and harmful actions or thoughts—goes against our nature.

Psalm 51 portrays a biblical picture of this necessary process. In this powerful psalm, King David confesses to God after his adultery with Bathsheba, which is recounted in 2 Samuel 11.

If it has been awhile since you've read David's song of broken confession, or if you've never read it before, consider taking a moment to read it now. You can feel David's sorrow and hear him own his actions as he tells God, "Against you, you only, have I sinned and done what is evil in your sight" (verse 4). Hear his plea for mercy and forgiveness: "Have mercy on me, O God, according to your unfailing love; according to your great compassion blot out my transgressions. Wash away all my iniquity and cleanse me from my sin" (verses 1-2).

And there is another side of the story that is often overlooked: God's broken heart. Second Samuel 12:7-8 gives us a glimpse into his sorrow. This passage provides such a vivid example of how hurting others hurts God, too: "This is what the Lord, the God of Israel, says, 'I anointed you king over Israel, and I delivered you from the hand of Saul. I gave your master's house to you, and your master's wives into your arms. I gave you the house of Israel and Judah. And if all this had been too little, I would have given you even more. Why did you despise the word of the Lord by doing what is evil in his eyes?'" God had given so much to David, yet in a moment of weakness, David forgot God and followed his passions. And that act shattered the heart of God, just as your sin and mine break his heart today. Scholar and writer Elie Weisel, who is a Holocaust survivor, makes this point powerfully when he writes of whom he calls the God of Kindness: "Watching your children suffer at the hands of your other children, haven't you also suffered?"[9]

When I turned to Christ, I did so because I urgently needed forgiveness and a way to start over again, and he provided. But I still need him today. Too often I still wander from the Lord's safe path. God only knows how I agree with the hymn-writer Robert Robertson:

O, to grace how great a debtor
  daily I'm constrained to be!
Let Thy goodness, like a fetter,
  bind my wandering heart to Thee:
Prone to wander—Lord I feel it—
  prone to leave the God I love;
Here's my heart—O take and seal it;
  seal it for Thy courts above.[10]

It is a miracle, this gift of forgiveness, unconditionally available to all of us who humbly confess sin and waywardness. It does not matter what the source of shame is. Name it: pornography, adultery, embezzlement, promiscuity, lying, substance abuse, an abortion, causing a divorce, cheating your way through college, or whatever else you may have contended with in the past or may still be contending with. Start by saying a simple, sincere, unvarnished prayer, such as, "God, you are right. I have sinned against you and others, even people whom I love very much. I was wrong, and I am deeply sorry." It takes grace and guts to whisper a prayer like that and take it to heart. That's our side of the equation. It is God's side to do what he promised: cleanse us and renew us.

For those who have suffered because of something that is truly an accident, it has been my experience that we still need to hand that day, that hour, that moment over to God. He sees how sorry we are, and he knows we are not necessarily at fault for what ended up happening. No matter what, know that God loves you and wants you to be free to receive his forgiveness right at the point of your greatest regret. "Oh, God! I have battled so many years with memories of that terrible day. I only wish I could take it all back. But I cannot. I cling to the hope that can come through your gift of forgiveness. Living with this guilt has robbed me of so much of my life. I hand it all over to you and embrace your forgiveness in exchange. Help me in the places where it is still hard to embrace forgiveness."

Believe It Sincerely

The second component to forgiving ourselves is to believe God's word and not our feelings. Being forgiven has nothing to do with *feeling* forgiven. A Bible study leader once told me that while forgiveness is based on Jesus' death on the cross, the *feelings* of forgiveness can take days, months, or even years to follow, depending on the severity of the offense. But while it may take time for our feelings to catch up, we are very much forgiven in God's eyes. And if God forgives us, we can forgive ourselves.

> "I, even I, am he who blots out your transgressions, for my own sake, and remembers your sin no more."

This isn't always easy to accept. Many times waves of shame and guilt continue to wash over me with sin and mistakes I have confessed and God has forgiven long ago. I have to go to the Scriptures and read passages on forgiveness out loud, thanking God and recognizing that his word is truer than my feelings of guilt. Then I *choose* to believe his words and not my feelings. A few of my favorite places to go when I am caught in the quagmire of shameful sorrow:

Psalm 103:10-13—*He does not treat us as our sins deserve or repay us according to our iniquities. For as high as the heavens are above the earth, so great is his love for those who fear him; as far as the east is from the west, so far has he removed our transgressions from us. As a father has compassion on his children, so the Lord has compassion on those who fear him…*

Isaiah 43:25—*I, even I, am he who blots out your transgressions, for my own sake, and remembers your sins no more.*

Colossians 1:13-14—*For he [God] has rescued us from the dominion of darkness and brought us into the kingdom of the Son he loves, in whom we have redemption, the forgiveness of sins.*

Another important fact to remember when it comes to receiving the forgiveness Jesus died to give us: We are in a spiritual war. "Our struggle is not against flesh and blood, but against the rulers, against the authorities, against the powers of this dark world and against the spiritual forces of evil in the heavenly realms" (Ephesians 6:12). Jesus' death not only granted us freedom from the bondage of our sin, but it represents a complete defeat to God's greatest adversary, Satan. If the devil cannot keep us from becoming followers of Christ, he wants to keep us from experiencing all that is ours as God's children. And at the top of that list is forgiveness.

In my experience, I have observed that many of us, even long-time followers of Jesus, can be consumed with guilt from past mistakes or even current struggles with sin. But instead of confessing, thanking God we're forgiven, and moving on in victory, we are held in bondage by the enemy of our souls. The ramification is that we can miss experiencing the benefits of knowing Christ as our Savior: love, joy, peace, and patience, to just name a few. We can be too quick to listen to evil whispers. I know this firsthand. Perhaps some of these thoughts sound familiar: "You've gone too far to be forgiven." "Don't kid yourself; God is keeping track of all your hurtful ways and even your accidental mistakes. And with each misdeed, he removes a portion of his love for you." "Face it;

you're not as welcome in his presence as you once were." Please know that such fleeting thoughts are deceptions, and nothing can come between you and God's lavish love and forgiveness.

To counteract these kinds of damaging messages and thoughts, I wholeheartedly recommend that people consider making consistent reading and meditating on God's word a part of their life and routine, if they aren't already. I made that decision years ago and have never regretted it.

Receive It Completely

This, by far, is the hardest aspect of forgiveness, to simply receive it as the gift it is meant to be. In John 8:31-32, Jesus utters the believer's Emancipation Proclamation, "If you hold to my teaching, you are really my disciples. Then you will know the truth, and the truth will set you free." *Oxford American Dictionary* defines *free* as "not a slave, not in the power of another or others, not fixed or held down, able to move around without hindrances."[11] Satan wants to hold us down and keep us bound up, as we have seen. But spiritual freedom is the birthright for all who have called on the name of the Lord.

Let's look at one more song penned by King David after his sin with Bathsheba, Psalm 32. Notice how David's way of achieving freedom from the grip of sin matches what I have been exploring. Verses 1-2 express David's joyful freedom through forgiveness: "Blessed is he whose transgressions are forgiven, whose sins are covered. Blessed is the man whose sin the Lord does not count against him and in whose spirit is no deceit." David has become the blessed man he is referring to, and he is free.

Following these great affirmations of freedom, David recalls the feelings of unforgiveness during the time he chose not to be honest and own his sin. If you do the math to see how long it took David to come to his spiritual senses and confess, it was almost nine months. So David lived in painful denial for quite some time. He gives us a graphic description of his agonizing life before his confession: "When I kept silent, my bones wasted away through my groaning all day long. For day and night your hand was heavy upon me; my strength was sapped as in the heat of summer" (verses 3-4).

That sounds all too familiar to me.

But then, at last, David made the right choice: "Then I acknowledged my sin to you and did not cover up my iniquity. I said, 'I will confess my transgressions to the Lord'—and you forgave the guilt of my sin" (verse 5).

David came to a place of believing he could be forgiven and then lived in such a way that he could receive it.

Another observation about Psalms 51 and 32 and King David's response as he chose to receive forgiveness: His sin was not just between him and God. He was the most powerful man in the land, so when he saw Bathsheba bathing and summoned her, I am not sure she had the right in that culture to refuse. Later, when she disclosed to David that she was pregnant, he ordered his military leader to send Bathsheba's husband, Uriah, to the frontlines of a battle so he would be killed. Suffice it to say David entangled himself deeply in a web of wrongdoing, and he had much for which to make amends. He had not only sinned against God, first and foremost, but he had sinned against others, too, with life-altering consequences. For each one, he had to own it deeply, believe God could forgive all he had done because of God's promises, and receive forgiveness completely. We can see in the Psalms evidence he did all of that, but it took a great deal of time.

When we walk through these steps and apply these principles, we can eventually, like David, emerge on the other side. And, we can be assured we will not be the same when we arrive there. We may have scars, and a part of us may never fully recover. But we *can* live forgiven.

None of us has to live haunted by our past or oppressed by something currently in our life. If we own our transgression, if we confess, repent, and be broken for breaking the heart of God

> ## "None of us has to live haunted by our past."

and perhaps the hearts of other people in our lives, we can, in time, find real freedom. Here is another compelling story about the beauty and wonder of receiving and embracing forgiveness.

Undressed and Undone

Ours was a good marriage with no signs of trouble.

We married later than most of our friends in the synagogue. I was 19 and my soon-to-be husband was 21. I shall never forget the week of boisterous, joyful celebrations. The atmosphere was electric with anticipation as all our friends and family joined in the merriment. The wedding ceremony was perfect in every way, our first evening alone, a bit awkward, but full of intimacy we knew would only grow over time. Our love blossomed, and our marriage strengthened. To this day, I wonder how it all went so tragically awry.

It was actually one of the leaders in our synagogue who suggested we help a new couple integrate into the community. Having the gift of hospitality, I was eager to oblige. Helping them find a home, establish a social network, and get the wife acclimated to the markets was not work for me. I liked her immediately, and her husband and mine seemed to have a great deal in common. I could see us all becoming long-term friends.

But more was going on than met the eye. I found myself attracted to my new friend's husband, to his leadership abilities and handsome face. Thoughts about him began to occupy too much space in my mind. After each meeting, I looked forward—too much—to seeing him again.

This is very hard to even admit, but there were secret side glances between my friend's husband and me, all very innocent to begin with, I promise you. But one evening, the four of us met for a meal together, and the greeting embrace between the two of us lasted a beat too long. I did not know it then—oh, how I did not know it then!—but we were on a slippery slope to a very dark, compromising place. How I wish I had just stopped there. Walked away. Never looked back.

But I didn't.

Identifying the steps that lead to an act of unfaithfulness is nauseously upsetting and humiliating: a line crossed by me here, another crossed by him there. Eventually, one day, one fateful day, he and I secretly planned to meet at his home, while both our spouses were away, to do what only a husband and wife do. I knew it was wrong, but I thought it would all stay quiet, undercover. No one would ever find out. I arrived as planned, and our pent-up passion took over.

At dawn the unthinkable happened.

The front door to his home burst open. We heard loud, angry voices calling out our names. How did anyone even know we were there? We heard fast footsteps heading for the bedroom. Horrified, I jumped from the bed and fell into an utter panic and disbelief, looking for any place to hide. But there was no place to escape. The door swung open. Before us stood the leaders of the synagogue, including the man who had introduced us just months ago. I was in the middle of a nightmare, fully awake.

"I was in the middle of a nightmare, fully awake."

The men grabbed me, naked, from the room and dragged me outside. I was so dazed, I failed to notice they took only me. Their hands touched me everywhere as they shoved me along toward God-knows-where. I was terrified and humiliated. Bystanders just beginning their daily routines stopped, stared, and gestured at me in shock. I recognized some of their faces and felt a shame I had never before imagined. Could anything be worse than this?

At last, the disgraceful procession stopped, and I found myself in the temple courts. As I tried in vain to shield myself with my hands, the men who had brought me to this place, religious leaders all, tossed me roughly to the ground in front of a stranger. Why was I here, of all places? And who was this man? Mortified, I buried my face in the dust at his feet.

One of the religious leaders yanked me to my feet, but I was too ashamed to make eye contact with the man before whom I now stood. But when I finally lifted my head and saw him, I recognized him. He was Jesus, the one many called "Messiah."

The First Journey: Embracing Forgiveness

I had heard much about this man: the miracles of healing the masses, how he touched lepers and loved children. A man of God. I myself had only seen him from a distance, but the people of Jerusalem could not stop talking about him. And now to meet him like this—there was no doubt in my mind he felt the same way about me as my accusers did. After all, he was a holy man, and everything they were saying about me was true. But the look on his face was vastly different from the accusing, hateful countenances of those who had brought me to him. I saw neither disdain nor condemnation in his eyes. Then an angry voice from among the circle of men demanded, "Teacher, this woman was caught in the act of adultery! In the Law of Moses, we are commanded to stone such a woman. Now, what do you say?"

I knew the answer before he had a chance to give it. I knew my life was over, that I would never get an opportunity to tell my husband how sorry I was. Words could not describe the depths of my remorse.

What happened next still does not make sense. He didn't speak at all. He bent down before me and began writing on the ground with his finger. Between the tears and the dust in my eyes, I had trouble making out what he was writing, but I had no trouble hearing the persistent, jeering questions from the religious leaders. I was frozen, fearful of moving. But Jesus was not. He stood up, faced the crowd, which quieted instantly in expectancy, and finally spoke with authority, "If any one of you is without sin, let him be the first to throw a stone at her." I could not breathe. I knew rocks were already in their hands, ready to be hurled in my direction. I shut my eyes and lowered my head. But no stones came. Instead, I heard the shuffling of feet *away* from me. Daring to look, I saw Jesus, bent down again, writing more words in the dust with his finger. And the slow exodus of my accusers continued, until within a few moments all were gone...except Jesus and me.

Jesus stood again, not to address a crowd, but to speak to *me*. He took off his robe, placed it around my shoulders so I could cover myself, and, with tenderness and grace, asked me two questions I will never forget: "Woman, where are they? Has no one condemned you?" In awe, I looked around the courtyard. It was empty. "No one, sir," I said.

I could not take my eyes off of his countenance, full of love. What he said next changed my life forever: "Then neither do I condemn you. Go now and leave your life of sin." Wilting, I buried my face in my hands and wept. I wept with thanksgiving. I had received forgiveness for my sin of adultery from one who clearly had the authority to condemn me and yet had forgiven me instead. I could not fully explain it, but even though he had spoken hard truth to me—leave my life of sin—at the same time, his words betrayed not one hint of hatred or contempt. I deserved to be punished, yet I had been forgiven and set free.

"Wilting, I buried my face in my hands and wept."

The rebuilding of my life and reputation was a long, hard process. My behavior—my sin—had broken my husband's heart, humiliated him, and nearly destroyed our marriage. Hurt, anger, and betrayal were giant barriers for him to overcome and forgive. I fully confessed to him and, in time, I received forgiveness not only from Jesus but, amazingly, from my husband, as well. I am eternally grateful to both.

With time and God's help, my relationship with my husband was transformed and restored—a miracle for which I'll always be thankful. It became clear to my husband I was changing, and a great deal of the change had to do with cultivating a relationship with the very one who first forgave me: Jesus. For years I had thought I didn't need the God I had been raised to believe in all my life, thinking I was a strong woman able to do the right things on my own. But my sin humbled me and opened my eyes to my weaknesses. Up to the point of my adultery, my relationship with God had been wooden and distant. No more! It became vital and close, like that of a child with her loving father.

My husband and I have had occasion to be in Jesus' company many times since that fateful morning. The Lord talks often about nothing being impossible with God. I have experienced this truth, and I hope you can, too.

—Adapted from John 8:1-11

Seeking Truth

The man who wrote most of the New Testament, the apostle Paul, possessed quite a reputation—not as a godly man, but as a murderous madman out to imprison Christian men and women for their faith. If we take a few moments to reflect on his life and the stunning transformation that occurred when he met Jesus, we can find worthwhile inspiration and encouragement.

Getting Context

Read Acts 6:8-15; 7:51-8:3; and 9:1-2.

- What was going on in the book of Acts at this time (Acts 6:8-15)?

- What was Saul doing at the time (Acts 8:3)?

- Using a little creative license, what do you think Saul was like at this time in his life?

- Was there a time in your life when you were resistant or even opposed to the message of Christ, as Saul was?

Saul's Conversion

Read Acts 9:3-18. The three main players in this scene are Jesus, Saul, and Ananias.

- List some of the miracles in the passage.

- Do you have a story of your coming to faith in Jesus like Saul's, albeit less dramatic?

A Changed Life

Read Acts 9:19-27.

- List the changes you see in Saul in this passage.

- What happened to Saul in Acts 13:9? Why?

- Read Acts 26:9-18. (It is one of two places in Acts where Paul gives his testimony of his conversion. The other is found in Acts 22:2-21, should you want to read it at another time.) What can you discover about his Damascus Road experience as he looked back on the day of his salvation?

- What are some ways God has changed your life?

Experiencing Forgiveness

Read 1 Timothy 1:12-17 and Titus 3:3-8.

- From these passages, what are the indicators that Paul had personally experienced forgiveness from the Lord?

- From these passages, as well as the ones we've already read, we know that Paul was called to preach the gospel among the very same people he'd been persecuting, arresting, and incarcerating. Early on in Acts 9, we read that the church in Damascus was astonished he'd been converted. In Acts 21 Paul went to Jerusalem. In both places he had persecuted the church prior to his conversion. Could there have been friends or family members in the audience when he spoke about Christ? Could they have confronted him? No one knows for sure, but it is not hard to believe it could have happened. How hard would it have been for Paul to forgive himself for the lives he had ruined and the families he had torn apart?

- What are the most difficult aspects of forgiving yourself for past mistakes, either done intentionally or unintentionally?

- How might Paul's example help all of us?

If you need more writing space, please feel free to use the blank pages near the end of the book (pages 110-115).

The Second Journey: Extending Forgiveness

Who Must I Forgive?

Returning hate for hate only multiplies hate, adding deeper darkness to a night already devoid of stars. Darkness cannot drive out darkness; only light can do that. Hate cannot drive out hate; only love can do that. Hate multiplies hate, violence multiplies violence, and toughness multiplies toughness in a descending spiral of destruction. So, when Jesus says, "Love your enemies," he is setting forth a profound and ultimately inescapable admonition.[12]

—Martin Luther King, Jr.

Almost Beyond Reach

At 10:45 in the morning on November 8, 1987, in the tiny Irish village of Enniskillen, something unthinkable and altogether horrific happened to Gordon Wilson. A soft-spoken, 60-year-old drapery maker, Wilson, his daughter Marie, and dozens of other families had gathered inside a bucolic church to honor war veterans when, without warning, a bomb detonated.

The force of the explosion destroyed the church and killed or wounded dozens of people. Buried within the smoldering rubble, Gordon Wilson and his daughter, a nurse, found each other's hands. Gordon did everything he could to will his daughter to stay alive, but Marie had been mortally wounded. He could only feel a profound sense of powerlessness as his daughter's strength ebbed, until she quietly slipped away.

The bombing, a grim milestone in the decades-long string of terrorist acts in Northern Ireland, claimed the lives of 12 people, including three married couples, dazing residents in the United Kingdom and bringing universal condemnation and rage. British Prime Minister Margaret Thatcher called it a "blot on mankind."[13]

Even so, in a tape-recorded interview with the BBC that can still be heard on the Internet, Gordon Wilson said and did something nearly as inconceivable as the bombing itself.

He first described in tragic detail his last conversation with Marie: "She held my hand tightly and gripped me as hard as she could. She said, 'Daddy, I love you very much.' Those were her exact words to me, and those were the last words I ever heard her say." Then, in the midst of his sorrow, he went on to say, "But I bear no ill will. I bear no grudge. Dirty sort of talk is not going to bring her back to life. She was a great lassie. She loved her profession. She was a pet. She's dead. She's in heaven and we shall meet again. I will pray for these men tonight—and every night."[14]

"But I bear no ill will. I bear no grudge."

His posture of forgiveness and grace towards his daughter's killers astonished and humbled people everywhere and kindled a forgiveness and reconciliation movement among young people in Ireland that remains active and vital to this day. Irish historian Jonathan Bardon said, "No words in more than 25 years of violence in Northern Ireland had such a powerful, emotional impact."[15]

I cannot imagine the inner anguish Gordon Wilson must have experienced nor how it is he managed to find his way to forgiveness in those circumstances.

I again am reminded of David and the somber passage in Psalm 60 where the once mighty king has sunk to such a devastatingly low moment in his life, that he says he feels as if God has abandoned him and may even be working against him. It was not true, but that was the way David felt. Somehow, at what must have been the lowest moment of his life, Gordon Wilson discovered within himself an ability to grant forgiveness. It's beyond extraordinary. It defies comprehension, really.

In the aftermath of the tragedy, which is recalled each year on Enniskillen Remembrance Day, Wilson became an influential public servant and politician known for his work as a peacemaker until his death in 1995. Because of his impact on both sides of the conflict, who knows how many lives were saved in subsequent years by Wilson's act of forgiveness?

Hopefully, none of us ever will be asked to suffer what Gordon Wilson endured, but losses of all manner are a part of life this side of Eden. And as profoundly difficult as it would be for any of us who is a parent to forgive someone who took the life of a son or daughter, I cannot think of a form of forgiveness that comes easily. Perhaps that is just me. There is often so much at stake. Our relationships and our lives are frequently complicated by indescribable wounded-ness and baggage, both real and perceived. And when it comes to forgiveness, our feelings often do not act as our allies.

As hard as forgiveness is to receive, it is even harder to give.

I have struggled to receive forgiveness, that is for sure. But my greatest personal battles in life have been in *extending* it to the ones who have hurt me.

I wish I could say otherwise.

Each of us, in our mind's eye, can probably conjure up faces of people who have betrayed us, lied to us, slandered us, abused us, or abandoned us. The memories may extend as far back as early childhood, elementary school, or the junior high years. They may include people who should have loved us the most—parents or other family members. Some are still alive, so there is hope to complete the circle of forgiveness with real reconciliation. Others have passed on, and so forgiveness cannot be fully extended because the all-important face-to-face conversations can never take place.

The late Catholic priest and writer Henri Nouwen lends wise insight: "We are all wounded people. Who wounds us? Often those whom we love and those who love us. When we feel rejected, abandoned, abused, manipulated, or violated, it is mostly by people very close to us: our parents, our friends, our spouses, our lovers, our children, our neighbors, our teachers, our pastors. Those who love us wound us too. That's the tragedy of our lives. This is what makes forgiveness from the heart so difficult. It is precisely our hearts that are wounded. We cry out, 'You, whom I expected to be there for me, you have abandoned me. How can I forgive you for that?'"[16]

Being in Christian ministry affords me multiple opportunities to hear story after story of people who have endured so much and are still trying to forgive—the report of a young woman drugged

> "We are all wounded people. Who wounds us? Often those whom we love and those who love us."

and raped by a schoolmate, the story of a boy abused by his camp counselor, the heart-breaking account of a woman returning home from work to find a Post-it note from her husband telling her he had never loved her and was leaving, or the description of a son being told by his father that he never wanted to see him again. So many life-changing and heart-wrenching encounters take place in our lives.

The Second Journey: Extending Forgiveness

Extending forgiveness is made possible because we have received it—first from God and then from others. Receiving forgiveness and learning to forgive ourselves form the foundation of forgiveness in our lives and fuel our capacity to forgive others. For most of us, the capacity to forgive others is essential if we are to become the people we want to be and the people God hopes we will become.

Throughout our lives, we tend to store up vivid memories of violent verbal exchanges and emotional confrontations. We remember names we were called, injustices we endured, the ways we were tossed aside and left behind. Oh, yes, we have memories.

When I was put up for adoption as a four-day-old infant, it was at a time when there was no such thing as an "open adoption," which allows for an adopted child to develop a relationship with her or his birth parents. Today, such arrangements are not uncommon. But I never met my birth mother, or saw a picture of her, or knew much of anything about her. My adoptive parents met her only once, for a brief moment, and they told me almost nothing—no physical description, no retelling of any conversation, almost no details.

I have always had so many unanswered questions about my heritage: What did my mother look like? How was she gifted? Who was my birth father? *Why didn't they want me?*

As I've talked with other adults who were adopted, it seems we fall into two camps. Some dream of the idyllic birth parents out there who want to track down the child they gave up, reunite with their child, and lavish this child with love. There is another camp, a darker, sadder one, one where the adopted ones assume the worst about the circumstances of their births, and I'm afraid I always fell into that group. I always wondered if I was the product of rape or incest or some other misfortune. The two details my parents did share with me about the day they brought me home were that my birth mother wore no ring on her finger and that no man was with her in the hospital room. So I came up with depressing scenarios to explain how she might have ended up pregnant. It all left me feeling unwanted, rejected, and unloved.

It has been a constant theme in my life that situations involving any sort of rejection have proven to be extremely emotional and difficult for me to handle.

I had always nursed deeply conflicted feelings about forgiving my birth mother, who was a source of my struggles with rejection. As a mother of two, I know what it is to carry and give birth to a baby. At the births of both of my children, Bryan and Brooke, I distinctly remember thinking of my birth mother and wondering how she could have given me away! It was inconceivable to me that you could give away your child to a virtual stranger. So I tended to tell myself that her life must have been so upside-down, she simply had no choice, that it was the only thing she could do. When I focused on that particular thought, I felt sorry for her lot in life.

But there was much more that needed to be resolved in my unforgiving soul.

There came a time when I went through an exercise of placing an empty chair in my back yard, imagining that my birth mother was sitting in it, and talking with her about how sad and angry I was that she didn't want me. Didn't she know I would have to deal with rejection all my life? Didn't she love me? And if so, how could she just hand me over to people she didn't even know? How did she know I would be safe or well cared for? Did *she* care?

I wept hard as I talked to that empty chair. But in the end, I knew I had to do what I have been talking to you about—forgive her from my heart. I unhooked the heavy chains that had bound us for decades and quit blaming her. I may have been an unwanted pregnancy, but I was not an unwanted child. Even as I write this, remembering that experience with the chair, I feel a heaviness. I have to remind myself that forgiveness, even after it has been given, is a process that can take a long time to fully play out. It is progressive. So, whenever I think of her and my important step towards closure with the chair exercise, I forgive her again and pray for her.

> ## "Didn't she know I would have to deal with rejection all my life? Didn't she love me?"

For me, the spiritual part of this played an enormous role in the act of forgiving my birth mother. When I became a follower of Christ, I learned from one of the books in the New Testament just how God feels about me. Ephesians 1:3-14 describes in great detail my new identity in Christ: I have been chosen by God; in love he has adopted me as his daughter; he has lavished me with grace; and he takes pleasure in me. Perhaps you can see how these words speak to the ugly undercurrent of rejection I've felt throughout my life. I am *wanted* in God's family; he does not *reject* me but has sent his son to die for my sins. I am forgiven, and so I can be with him for all eternity. That translates into *love* for me, and I have gone back to this truth about my new heritage countless times, year after year after year. On that difficult day in my back yard, it was strong enough to help me sincerely forgive my birth mother. I found a new place for her in my heart.

I thought that would be the end of the story.

But some time after going through the exercise of extending forgiveness to my birth mother, my friend Renee, who would be a private investigator if she were not already gainfully employed, asked me one day if she could try to find my birth mother for me.

I had never wanted to do that, for a host of reasons. But, to my own surprise, I said, "Sure," gave her what little information I had, and let her go to work on the search.

On a Saturday night in April 2008, everything changed.

I checked my email before heading to bed and noticed something from the California Department of Social Services. I just knew it contained valuable information about my adoption. Not wanting to read it alone, I asked my husband, Bob, to come into my home office, and I sat down in a comfortable chair to listen as he read the notice to me.

Instantly, my greatest fears were relieved. Amazingly, there was an entire page of information about both of my birth parents and the circumstances of my identity, all dictated to a nurse by my birth mother, who had included many of the specifics I had hungered to know my entire life!

I was numb.

For the first time, I knew *something* about my origins. What struck me immediately was that my birth mother was speaking to me personally, almost as if she knew I would read it one day! The pronouns "you" and "your" are laced throughout the document. She was 31 years old when she gave birth to me and had only been living in California for two months at the time of my birth. She was of Swedish descent, born in Washington State, and employed as a personnel clerk in a bank. She was five feet, six inches tall and had very blond straight hair, blue eyes, and a fair complexion. She and my birth father had known each other for a long period of time. They were friends who crossed the line one night, intimate only once, and I was conceived. As I heard this story, so very different from the one I had always imagined, I felt immediate relief that my beginning had not been in an act of violence or hurt, but in love. I never thought I'd be hearing such a thing.

I found out my mother and I had something in common, too.

She, like me, had to deal with rejection in her life. According to the documents, even though my birth father was informed of the pregnancy, he married someone else just three weeks before my birth.

I will quote what moved me most: "Your birth mother placed you for adoption as she knew that you were in a good home, and felt that even if she married in the future, it would be much better for you to be adopted."

She *had* thought about me. She *had* loved me. She *had* wanted the best for me.

This information soothed such a long-wounded spirit within me and enabled me to extend forgiveness in a far more personal way—to a blond-haired, blue-eyed woman who did what she thought was best.

> "Unforgiveness can erode us into people we do not want to be."

Unforgiveness can erode us into people we do not want to be. We can live an awfully long time with currents of anger and bitterness running deep within us.

The longer we walk through the museum of our memories and allow ourselves to linger longest at the worst ones without coming to terms with them, the more unforgiveness can undermine our lives. I am reminded of writer Anne Lamott's wry observation that "not forgiving is like drinking rat poison and then waiting for the rat to die."[17]

The freedom of forgiveness is unlike any other. It allows us to put others and ourselves in a place of great compassion. Without it, we put ourselves in the position of becoming our own worst enemies.

Let me tell you of another dear friend, Laura, who has recently been forced to confront the caustic forces of unforgiveness that can so invisibly influence us.

Not long ago Laura and her best friend, Jan, were on the telephone together when Jan suddenly confronted Laura. "You have become an angry person," she said. "Your anger is like something you put on each day before you go out into the world, like an old pair of jeans." Laura was startled. Here are her own words about that crucial day:

> I was shocked and hurt. I started to cry. But almost immediately, I knew my friend was right. For far too long, I had been seething inside. I was so angry with my father, I had even found it impossible to call this man, a man for whom I had always had such a deep well of affection, my "Daddy."

A jarring revelation and series of events had shattered Laura's relationship with her father, and Laura was consumed with bitterness.

A few years earlier and only a few months after her mother had been diagnosed with stage four breast cancer, Laura had been visiting her parents when a knock came at the door. She answered it, and an unfamiliar man asked to see her mother. Laura awakened her mother from a nap and, after spending an hour on the porch talking with this man, Laura's mom revealed that the man was the husband of a woman who had been having an affair with Laura's father.

In that moment, the strong fortress of warmth, love, and solidarity that had marked her family throughout Laura's childhood crumbled—a devastating blow to her image of the man she had always adored and idolized, her Daddy.

And, in time, things would only get worse.

> Over the next three years, my parents attempted to mend their relationship, even as Mom's health deteriorated and it became apparent she was not going to make it. I honestly think she stayed with him only because she didn't want to die alone.

Laura tried her best to be there for them, and the situation was improved by the fact that her mother decided to become a Christian and, soon after, so did her father.

> I think after so much pain of trying to juggle two lives, my dad finally realized he needed divine help. It was a glorious thing to see my dad accept Christ and grow in his newfound faith. But within a few months, his enthusiasm for God seemed to wane, and there were signs that my father was returning to his former ways.

Laura was right. Inside, her anger and disappointment slowly gathered, even as she tried to put on a pleasant face for the sake of her dying mother.

Ten days after her mother's death, Laura would learn that her father had secretly boarded a plane to go see his mistress.

Ten months after her mother's passing, the mistress moved into her mother's home and became Laura's stepmother.

One afternoon, after repeated requests, Laura finally agreed to meet with her stepmother, who begged her, through tears, for forgiveness.

Laura's response? A firm, flat "No."

> I had been through too much. The pain and anger were just too great. I simply did not have within me the ability to forgive.

That exchange took place an hour before the fateful phone call when Laura's best friend confronted her about the intense anger that had come to infect so much of her life, an anger that was even embittering her own four children.

> Through my friend, I sensed God's lead that I had been wrong, that I needed to extend forgiveness or I would be putting at risk much of my own life and my children's. I suddenly knew what needed to be done.

> I realized that even though my dad and his mistress did not deserve my forgiveness, I could not possibly refuse to extend something to others that had been so graciously given to me. Did this feel right? No. Did I want to do this? No. Would this be the hardest spiritual decision of my life? Yes. But I knew it had to be done.

Laura recently met with her father and her stepmother and began the process of extending forgiveness.

How are things going in their relationship? It's not perfect. There is definite progress, but it is halting. It depends on the day or sometimes even the hour.

But there is also an unmistakable freedom for Laura because the disappointment, anger, and resentment that had been operating

> "I could not possibly refuse to extend something to others that had been so graciously given to me."

silently below the surface of her existence and contaminating her relationships have been called out. She stood up to them, named them for what they were, faced them, and took decisive, solid steps towards the healing process.

There is a sense that something new has begun. And with this sense of something new comes a sliver of hope, then another, then another.

Like Laura, I have gone down the path of letting unforgiveness mark me for way too long. I know the terrain all too well. It is an arduous journey to be able to extend forgiveness, but both Laura and I can honestly say it can genuinely free our souls and alter the trajectory of our lives.

The Circles of Forgiveness

In life there are three different domains, or circles, where we need to be pro-active in dealing with extending forgiveness to others. Some paths towards extending forgiveness are easier to navigate than others, but all are critical.

The Clean Circle of Forgiveness: This circle represents day-in-day-out forgiveness. A roommate leaves the kitchen in a mess after you cleaned it up the night before, a mother has a harsh word with her child, a husband deposits his clothes on the floor *again*, or your mother-in-law forgets your birthday. These are maddening events that can aggravate and exasperate us. But clean forgiveness can happen between emotionally healthy people who don't absorb every little infraction as a personal attack. So, when you approach the offending person or persons about a hurtful comment, action, or inaction, they are freer to take responsibility and offer a sincere apology.

There is a mutual, two-way giving and receiving of forgiveness by all parties. Denial, blame-shifting, and finger-pointing are checked at the door of the clean circle of forgiveness. There is healing in the exchange and even a deepening of the relationship because you've had to go to a sensitive place and emerge out the other side with a stronger bond. This requires humility and teach-ability on both sides. Once more, I am in no way suggesting it is easy, because extending forgiveness is *never* easy. But when the breach is talked about in a timely manner, anger, bitterness, and a desire for retaliation are denied an opportunity to grow.

How can we live in the clean circle of forgiveness? First, by acknowledging we will be both victim *and* perpetrator with forgiveness throughout our lives. It is an inevitable reality. We will likely need to extend and receive forgiveness on a daily basis. It can become a part of our lifestyle, this presumption of grace and forgiveness towards others.

Living in the clean circle of forgiveness demands we hold certain truths in balance. We have to be honest and humble. If we are the ones who have violated a boundary, we need to avoid being defensive and admit our mistake, both to God and to the person whom we have offended. If we can learn to accept forgiveness graciously when it is offered and extend it when it is needed, we will benefit greatly.

This leads me to a second vital aspect of life in the clean circle of forgiveness: It has a strong spiritual element to it. I have mentioned this before, but it bears repeating. If you know Jesus as your personal Savior, you have been a recipient of the matchless gift of forgiveness.

I *kind of* knew this when I became a follower of Christ in college, but the more I've lived my life and hurt people I love, the more I am aware of my need to stay in touch with the fact that I have been forgiven a *lot* and need to forgive others because of that reality.

Jesus forgave others throughout his ministry. Perhaps the most poignant occurrence was when he forgave the once-taunting thief

> "Jesus, fully God, took on human flesh and bone for primarily one reason: to forgive you and me."

on the cross. Jesus looked beyond the behavior and forgave this now-repentant man. He forgave harlots, fishermen, rabbis, and the religious elite for all of the ways in which they all so desperately needed forgiveness. Jesus, fully God, took on human flesh and bone for primarily one reason: to forgive you and me. As a Christian, the more I can enfold my mind and heart around this truth, the cleaner my forgiveness will be.

The apostle Paul addressed this spiritual dimension of forgiveness. Ephesians 4:31-32 is pretty clear: "Get rid of all bitterness, rage and anger, brawling and slander, along with every form of malice. Be kind and compassionate to one another, *forgiving each other, just as in Christ God forgave you*" (Italics added). And again in Colossians 3:13 we read, "Bear with each other and forgive whatever grievances you may have against one another. *Forgive as the Lord forgave you*" (Italics added). Meditating on what these principles look like for each of us can help us live well inside the clean circle of forgiveness.

The Complicated Circle of Forgiveness: This describes where we encounter most of the difficulty in extending forgiveness in our lives. *Oxford American Dictionary* defines *complicated* as "made up of many parts, difficult to understand or use because of this; complex."[18] There is nothing clean about this kind of forgiveness. It is multifaceted, convoluted, and chuck full of toxic emotions.

Like the painful example in my friend Laura's life, the triggering event or events that typically land us in the complicated circle of forgiveness probably happened months, years, or even decades ago. In spite of the passage of time, we hold onto graphic memories of being blamed and punished for something we never did, of a best friend turned worst enemy, of someone's spreading false rumors about us, of being unfairly fired from a job, of being taken advantage of, or worse, by someone we have loved and trusted, and the list goes on and on. Perhaps there was an attempt to reconcile, but it was brushed aside or ignored altogether or met with hostility. Author and teacher Max Lucado writes: "No doubt you've had your share of words that wound. You've felt the sting of a well-aimed gibe. Maybe you're still feeling it. Someone you love or respect slams you to the floor with a slur or a slip of the tongue. And there you lie, wounded and bleeding. Perhaps the words were intended to hurt you, perhaps not; but that doesn't matter. The wound is deep. The injuries are internal. Broken heart, wounded pride, bruised feelings. Or maybe your wound is old. Though the arrow was extracted long ago, the arrowhead is still lodged…hidden under your skin. The old pain flares unpredictably and decisively, reminding you of harsh words yet unforgiven."[19]

So, what do we do in this situation? We want to live in a place of forgiveness, like my friend Laura, but how can we forgive someone who doesn't want it, will not recognize the need for forgiveness, and has no plans of ever even acknowledging the offense?

> "Someone you love or respect slams you to the floor with a slur or a slip of the tongue. And there you lie, wounded and bleeding."

These are haunting but real questions for us living in the complicated circle of forgiveness. They're highly personal conversations for me. It has been in the complicated circle of forgiveness that I've lived for most of my life. God, in his grace, has taught me a little about how to forgive when the other party does not want to. I only wish I applied it more often. Remember, there is a selfish component to the need to extend forgiveness when it has not been asked for or wanted: I don't want the poison of unforgiveness to make *me* into a bitter and angry woman. We can falsely believe our unforgiveness is hurting the offender, but in reality it is only hurting us. Forgiveness releases us to live again in a special brand of freedom. Theologian Saint Augustine captures the power of this kind of life when he says, "Forgiveness is the remission of sins. For it is by this that what has been lost, and was found, is saved from being lost again."[20]

When I forgive a person who has wronged me, I am unhooking the destructive bungee cord that keeps me bound to the offense and to the offender. As you know, a bungee cord has hooks on both ends with an elasticized rope between. When I choose to live in the place of unforgiveness, I stay fastened to the worst memories I have. I can think I have gotten over the infraction and have moved on with my life, but when I hear a song that reminds me of the incident or see a picture, that toxic bungee cord snaps me right back to the event as if it happened yesterday. One major way out of the complicated circle of forgiveness is to un-tether ourselves once and for all via heartfelt forgiveness. Here again, Richard Foster echoes my feelings on the topic: "Forgiveness means that this real and horrible offense shall not separate us. Forgiveness means that we will no longer use the offense to drive a wedge between us, hurting and injuring one another. Forgiveness means that the power of love that holds us together is greater than the power of the offense that separates us. That is forgiveness. In forgiveness we are releasing our offenders so that they are no longer bound to us. In a very real sense we are freeing them to receive God's grace. We are also inviting our offenders back into the circle of fellowship."[21]

> "Forgiveness means this real and horrible offense shall not separate us."

Jesus gave us very sensible ways to practice forgiveness in the complicated circle. The principles in Luke 6:27-28 have been life-changing for me: "But I tell you who hear me: Love your enemies, do good to those who hate you, bless those who curse you, pray for those who mistreat you." I have learned to love my enemies by blessing them and praying for them. Let me elaborate.

Formerly, when the faces of "enemies" came into my mind, I had always cursed them, carried on imaginary arguments with them (which I always won), or imagined any number of horrible things befalling them. This is a justifiable option for people who wish to stay securely locked in the complicated circle. But I have learned to make significant changes in the way I respond to resurfacing pain. One speaker I heard years ago put it this way: "I cannot change my past, but by God's grace I can be free from it"—free from the pain, free from the bondage, and free to know joy and peace again. To achieve this freedom, I apply the principles of the Luke passage both critically and progressively. By this I mean that I forgive my offenders at a critical moment in time but progressively make choices in how I respond to the memories that continue to flare up. Now, when unpleasant memories and enemies' faces come back to mind, tempting me toward bitterness and retaliation, I look those faces *in* the face and pray blessings on them and their loved ones. "Lord, bless their relationships (and then I will name some of them specifically), bless them financially and emotionally, but mostly bless them with a deeper, sweeter walk with you." I also *act* in loving ways. I call, email, send birthday gifts, and speak to them kindly. Henri Nouwen again articulates this so well, "You will be delighted to discover that you can no longer remain angry with people for whom you've really and truly prayed. You will find that you start speaking differently to them or about them, and that you're actually willing to do well to those who've offended you in some way."[22] I progressively do this in order to continue to live in a place of unconditional love and forgiveness, steering clear of the complicated circle.

Now, this is not about writing "welcome" on my back and lying down, thus granting permission for people to walk all over me. Nor does extending forgiveness mean I will forget the hurt or abuse, nor is it looking the other way, nor is it imagining that the betrayal never happened.

Letting people who have hurt me off the hook has built my character and increased my love and devotion to the one who forgave me. I am more whole because I have forgiven offenders. I have relished the rare times in my life when my relationship with a person has moved from the more complicated circle of forgiveness to the more navigable clean circle. It is a healing and life-giving experience.

I have another very personal and dramatic story that illustrates how this can happen. My mother-in-law, Cora, was raised in a very difficult, even abusive, home. She understandably entered adulthood emotionally unprepared for the challenges of life. Early on she made some poor choices that reaped a lifetime of anguishing consequences. She was an alcoholic.

As a young boy, Bob told his mother he would help her stop drinking, but she ignored him. It would be decades before she would address the problem. Our relationship with her was an odd combination of enjoyment and difficulty. A prickly side of her often came out when she visited us. Finally, she had reached her fifties when a crisis hit that prompted her to make the brave decision to go into rehab. After a month, she was free of the burden she had carried for years. We were so very proud of her. And the healing began.

"It is worth the pain in order to be set free."

She was happier and more enjoyable to be with. But the *real* change occurred when she was 80 years old. Hospitalized for a drug interaction, she feared she was about to die. We had talked with her for years about beginning a relationship with Jesus. Although polite in her refusal, she had wanted no part of religion. She always expressed gladness that it "worked for us" but saw no need on her end. But alone one night in the ICU, she underwent a remarkable change of heart in her advanced age. She knew if she died she would be alone for all eternity, and she cried out to Jesus in prayer. She told us later, amid tears, that he reassured her she would never be alone and would be with him in heaven. We had prayed for her for 30 years. When we received the phone call detailing this amazing turn of events, we were floored and filled with joy.

We quickly arranged a visit for her to our home in Florida. She was still not well but was determined to see us. As soon as she arrived, she wanted to talk with Bob and me privately. She told us of her *nightly* battle with the memory of her little boy sitting across the counter, begging her to quit drinking. She had been free of the burden of alcoholism for decades but carried another burden, the need to experience forgiveness from the one she had hurt. She burst into tears and asked for Bob's forgiveness. It was a moment we shall never forget. Bob had forgiven her long ago, but the conversation was extremely healing for him. He could tell her he forgave her, and she could see how sincere it was. Something in him had finally been settled that evening. The remnants of a childhood wound were now completely healed.

And the transition happened—a long-needed forgiveness migrated from the complicated circle to the clean one.

Cora passed away just a few years later. But we know where she is. And we shall see her again.

In the Lord's Prayer, Jesus teaches us how to pray. One aspect of the prayer is forgiveness, the kind we experienced that amazing evening with Cora: "Forgive us our debts, as we also have forgiven our debtors" (Matthew 6:12). This charge reminds me of the wonderful mechanics of forgiveness. It comes into me, and it travels out from me. I must breathe it in, and I must let it out. Bible teacher Dr. Charles Stanley's insight gives me hope: "If you live with events in your past that are painful to even think about, please accept by faith that it is worth the pain in order to be set free. And whatever scar may be felt will be much easier to live with than the open wound you now bear."[23]

The Closed Circle of Forgiveness: The circle in this category is closed because the ones to whom we need to extend forgiveness are no longer in our lives and maybe never were. I call them the Unseen Ones—the father you never knew, the birth mother (like mine) who put you up for adoption as a newborn, or your mom who just walked out one day to "follow her dreams" and left you with a nightmare of a life. The ones who need your forgiveness may have died or moved away or simply made themselves permanently unavailable to you. These people occupy our closed circle of forgiveness because they are not *here* to receive the forgiveness we need to extend so we can go on in wholeness.

Lewis Smedes unpacks this concept so well when he writes, "Some people invade our lives for a tragic hour or a sad lifetime, leave us with hurting memories, and then move away where we cannot see them. They are invisible, people whose reality is now woven from the thin fabric of a time that no longer is. They are no less real to us than people we see before us, people with faces and names and bodies to touch. They are only harder to reach with our hands and with our forgiveness."[24]

I am struck by the phrase *only harder to reach with our forgiveness*. Not impossible, not unattainable, not unachievable, only harder.

Many of us have Unseen Ones in our lives. This was precisely the case with my birth mother. And it is my hope that my sharing what happened—and the incredible and unexpected healing I experienced—might enable you to extend forgiveness to the very ones you may have thought of at the beginning of this second journey to forgiveness. For now, enjoy a look at a very complicated circle of forgiveness and how one young man found his way to a remarkable gesture of extending forgiveness. As you read this story, perhaps you may see yourself somewhere in the narrative and maybe even be compelled to think of someone who probably secretly longs for, and fiercely needs, your forgiveness.

Forgiveness at Long Last

To say I was raised in an unusual home would be an understatement.

My father had not one wife, but four. None of them got along with one another. Fighting, manipulating, and back-stabbing characterized the relationships among these women for as long as I can remember. They constantly jockeyed for my father's attention and affection. From my earliest days, I knew it was a dysfunctional family, but I had no idea how much worse things would get.

> **"To say I was raised in an unusual home would be an understatement."**

I was the first of two sons my mother bore in my father's old age. I could never prove it, but I think my mom was my dad's favorite wife. What I did know, beyond any doubt, was I was his favorite child. I was in my mid-teens when he made me the most beautiful, brilliantly colored tunic. I was shocked when he presented it to me, since no other sibling had one like it. Every time I put it on I felt the love of my father. It was the most valuable possession I owned. Unfortunately, it became a constant reminder to my brothers that they did not have a coat like mine. Real trouble was brewing and I was unaware of it. What started as a glorious gift became a profound curse.

The whole mess started innocently enough, or so I thought. One day, I was with my brothers tending the family sheep herd. It was no easy task tending sheep, and everyone had his part to play in the work. The problem was my brothers were more interested in bickering among themselves, so the animals got ignored. That evening I told my father what had gone on in the pasture, and he was pretty angry at my brothers for not doing what was expected. That was a turning point for our family. From that day on, my brothers' simmering jealousy turned into overt animosity. They would not speak to me at all if possible, and if they had to, it was in a cutting, surly manner. I suppose it didn't help that I told my brothers and my father about two very odd dreams I had at the time. The dreams symbolically featured me, the second-youngest child, as the head of our household, leading everyone, including my father! In our culture, such a dream was highly disrespectful. In hindsight, I should have kept my mouth shut. But, as God is my witness, I really did have the dreams, and I told my family about them with no malice in mind.

If I had to sum up how my brothers felt about me, it would be hate. They were jealous and angry with me and had been for some time. It wasn't long before hate erupted into an act from which it would take years for our family to recover: My brothers actually plotted to kill me. Had my brother, Reuben, not intervened, I would have lost my life that day. He talked the other brothers into just throwing me into a deep pit, while he secretly planned to come rescue me later that day. But that rescue never came. While Reuben was away, another brother, Judah, suggested to the rest of the guys to sell me as a slave to a tribe of wandering nomads, and they did!

I found it hard to believe they were doing this to me. It wasn't until years later that I learned what happened after I was sold. These "brothers" actually took the ornamented coat my father made for me, covered it with goat's blood, and delivered it to my aging father, telling him I'd been devoured by wild animals. Seems they hated him, too. He mourned me as dead. It breaks my heart to recall what this deceitful lie did to my beloved father.

As I traveled with people who did not speak my language, I had a lot of time to talk with God. I was a young man but had learned about the God of my father from an early age. I knew he was real and had uniquely chosen our family and planned to bless the world through us. I loved and trusted this God, so when these outlandish things happened to me, I wondered just where God was in it all. It's hard for me to fully explain how God met me in that caravan, but he did. I had a heavenly reassurance that his favor was upon me, that he had not left me, and that a plan far more grand than I could imagine was unfolding *in* the evil my brothers had done to me.

"I wondered just where God was in it all."

On the other hand, I was dealing with a great deal of anger, hurt, and betrayal. I admit I'd been unwise and immature, but I had done nothing to merit the kind of treatment these family members had doled out to me. I was just seventeen years old. And these older brothers had just sold me off like the sheep we tended. I was nobody to them, and that seriously wounded my spirit. I had looked up to my brothers and loved them, but it was very clear they did not feel the same. There were a lot of tears shed on my journey to God-knows-where. It was an emotional season in my young life, knowing God was with me in this drama but being faced with very real feelings of retaliation and unforgiveness. I was in a real tug-of-war in my soul. God grasped one end of the rope, reminding me of his love and presence, while my raging emotions gripped the other end, tempting me to stay in a place of anger and unforgiveness. I began to learn early lessons about extending forgiveness to undeserving people. I stress "I *began* to learn." As you shall see, there would be many more hard forgiveness lessons for me to discover.

This tribe of Arabian merchants was headed to Egypt, I discovered well into my journey. When we arrived, I was sold as a slave to Potiphar, one of the officers in Pharaoh's court. It was probably the best place I could have ended up, all things considered. Potiphar immediately liked me and quickly entrusted his household to me. It was a great reassurance of God's love for me in this foreign place. And then the unthinkable happened: Potiphar's wife attempted to seduce me. I fled the house that day to escape her advances. Angry and spiteful, she concocted some wild story that I tried to rape her. By the end of the day, Potiphar had imprisoned me for something I never did. I was beginning to see a theme in my life: What was God up to with this turn of events? I sure didn't know the answer. Again, I had done nothing wrong. Yet I was still headed for prison. The tug-of-war was back with a vengeance. Live with resentment and a burning desire for revenge, or release the whole event into God's care? I wish I could say it was an easy choice. Hardly. But since God had previously granted me the grace to keep forgiving my brothers, it was a bit easier this time around. I just knew the Lord was the only one in this world I could trust. So, I did; I trusted him. God gave me faith beyond my years.

Well, the same drill happened in prison that had first happened in Potiphar's house. I found favor with the jailer, and he entrusted all the prisoners to my care. If I had not lived this life, I would not have believed this could be happening to me—again.

During my time in prison, God showed me a special gift he'd given to me, the ability to interpret dreams. I did it twice for two of my fellow prisoners, Pharaoh's former butler and baker, and my interpretations proved to be true.

A few years later, Pharaoh had two very disturbing dreams and sought out magicians and wise men from all over Egypt to interpret them, but they didn't have a clue. The butler, who had since been released from prison and was back in the employ of Pharaoh, remembered how I had understood his dream and suggested to his boss that I be asked to help—God's favor again displayed in my life. I was taken out of my prison cell and ushered into the presence of Pharaoh himself. God granted me the ability to interpret the two dreams. One dream foretold seven years of plenty in Egypt and the other dream foretold seven years of famine. I suggested to him that he find a man of good character to manage the years of plenty so Egypt could survive the years of poverty. He chose *me* right then and there and gave me almost unlimited authority! I was a foreigner, a slave, and a convict; I had no business being chosen to be second only to Pharaoh. Once again, it was God's hand of blessing on my life.

> **"Just seeing their cunning faces conjured up all kinds of memories—awful, painful memories."**

The next fourteen years were intense. I married, had two sons, and managed the country's seven years of prosperity in light of what was to come, the predicted seven years of famine. I conserved and stored up so much grain, that when the scarcity began, I was prepared not only to feed the people of Egypt, but by God's grace, to actually help supply food to the surrounding nations. And you will never guess who showed up in front of me one day well into the famine, asking for food. My brothers! Only my youngest brother, Benjamin, had stayed home with our father. They did not recognize me after all the years, but I knew in an instant who they were. Just seeing their cunning faces conjured up all kinds of memories—awful, painful, cruel memories.

Immediately the inner tug-of-war began again. I had their very lives right in the palms of my hands. I controlled all of the food supplies. I could easily have refused them—let them feel a dose of the desperation, rejection, and fear I'd lived with for over twenty years. But then I heard the voice of the Lord I had learned to recognize since leaving home. God had become my father, my friend, the one who forgave me of my sin, my constant companion through all the ups and downs of my life. At that very moment he reminded me of the dreams he'd given me as a teenager, the ones that foreshadowed a time when my brothers and father would bow down to me. And now, here were my brothers right in front of me, bowing down. I began to wonder, *Could this all be a part of God's plans to save our family? Has God allowed all the crushing events of my life just for this moment in time?* Although I remembered their cruelty, I forgave my brothers—again.

However, I had no plans to simply hand them the food they requested. I wanted to learn how much they had changed and grown as men since their heartless act toward me decades ago. I longed to see if this quarreling bunch of siblings could get along and finally do the right thing. And I yearned to know about my father's health and about my brother Benjamin. I spoke to them harshly and accused them of being spies. They groveled at my feet, claiming their innocence. But while I was devising my plan, I actually heard them speak about *me*. They, of course, didn't know I could understand them since they spoke in Hebrew, but what they said was, "Surely we are being punished because of our brother. We saw how distressed he was when he pleaded for his life, but we would not listen; that's why this distress has come upon us." Reuben replied, "Didn't I tell you not to sin against the boy? But you wouldn't listen; now we must give an accounting for his blood." I promise you, I heard sorrow, regret, and remorse in their voices. They had changed, I could see it.

I put them through a few more tests to be certain this change was real. I was amazed to discover that even Judah, the one who had been the most heartless toward me, was a completely different person. I could not believe the new heart of compassion I heard from him. I became fully persuaded of my brothers' repentance and equally thankful I had chosen to forgive them.

I finally, uncontrollably, blurted out, "I am Joseph! Is my father still alive?" They looked like they had seen a ghost! These once confident brothers were clearly terrified. They knew I could have them all killed in a moment, and I'm sure that's what they expected. But I told them God had sent me here to save our family and all who would come after us. What they had done in evil, God had used for good.

The reunion we had was full of tears, but nothing like the one with my father a few weeks later. Within a short period of time, my whole family relocated to Egypt so they could survive the years of famine still ahead. God's ways are not our ways.

—*Adapted from Genesis 37-50*

Obtaining Clarity

The Bible is filled with thoughts on the topic of extending forgiveness.

Extending Forgiveness: Jesus' Example

As we have already seen and will continue to study in this section, Jesus not only taught on forgiveness, he extended it time and again. Read each of the following accounts and note his words extending forgiveness and who it was he forgave. Is there a person with whom you identify most?

- Matthew 9:1-7

- Luke 7:36-39, 44-50

- Luke 23:32-43

- John 8:1-11

Extending Forgiveness: Who Do You Need to Forgive?

We have talked quite a bit in the second journey about whom exactly you need to forgive. The Bible makes some suggestions in the following passages. Who needs your forgiveness, according to these verses? Are they in your complicated or closed circle of forgiveness? Can you find it within yourself to forgive them?

- Psalm 27:10

- Psalm 55:12-14

- Luke 23:34-39

– Acts 7:54-60

Extending Forgiveness: It's Not Optional

These passages get straight to the heart of the matter of forgiving or not forgiving. Jesus is black and white on this topic, so I will let him do the talking. What does Jesus say in each passage? Explain, to your best ability, why Jesus makes the correlation between being forgiven and then extending forgiveness.

– Matthew 6:14-15

– Mathew 18:21-35

– Luke 6:37

Extending Forgiveness: It Is Possible

I have tried to stay hopeful throughout this second journey toward forgiveness. That is not easy because we have been talking about some of the worst things that have ever happened to us. Yet, forgiveness is possible. Let's take another look at two passages I have already referenced. Read them from a few

Grace & Guts

different translations or paraphrases (*New Living Translation* or *The Message*) and consider journaling your thoughts and feelings and processing your thinking with a trusted friend.

– Ephesians 4:31-32

– Colossians 3:12-14

If you need more writing space, please feel free to use the blank pages near the end of the book (pages 110-115).

The Third Journey:
Personalizing Forgiveness

Where Am I in the Forgiveness Process?

Only the brave know how to forgive; it is the most refined and generous pitch of virtue human nature can arrive at.[25]

—Laurence Sterne

At 73 years of age and with his eyesight failing, Alvin Straight has decided he is done with a lifetime of being prideful and stubborn, and he is telling a stranger why he is driving a lawn mower 300 miles from Iowa to Wisconsin to see his dying brother, to whom he has not spoken in a decade: "My brother and I said some unforgivable things last time we were together. I want to put those times behind us. This trip is just one hard swallow of pride. I'm only hopin' I'm not too late."

Prohibited from driving a car because of his poor vision, and refusing to take a bus because he doesn't trust other people to drive him, Straight, humbled by life, has set out with his riding mower and a trailer filled with gasoline and hot dogs, and he is determined to right a wrong with his brother Lyle. He reveals that things weren't always like this between them: "He and I used to sleep out in the yard every summer night it wasn't pouring. After nine months of winter we couldn't get enough of summer. We'd bunk down as soon as the sun went down and lie there talkin' ourselves to sleep. Talk about the stars…and other planets, whether there might be other people like us out there, 'bout all the places we wanted to go…made our trials seem smaller. We pretty much talked each other through growin' up."

He pauses and then laments, "Whatever it was made me and Lyle so mad doesn't matter to me now…I want to make peace…I want to sit with him again and look up at all the stars."

These touching scenes come from *The Straight Story*, a film based on a true story about the lengths a man is willing to go to in order to embrace and extend forgiveness. It packs a powerful message built around our need for atonement and the deepest yearnings of our souls. I do not want to spoil the ending, but it is as profound a message as any about the power of forgiveness in our lives, when Lyle, upon realizing how far Alvin has traveled and how he has done so, asks, "Did you ride that thing all the way here to see me?"

In the third journey, I am hoping we can embark on a somewhat similar quest—to begin to commit to a *life* of forgiveness, to personalize the principles and truths we have been absorbing together.

Christians dwell in this odd reality of being citizens of two very different places, of heaven and of earth. We know that Christ died for us. And because of that, we can embrace forgiveness. But we also live in *this* world. And we must come to terms with all of the emotions of this world. Part of what we must learn to do is to meld these two worlds with increasing degrees of grace, for ourselves and for others. How do we do that? So many tricky emotions bubble up from our past and our present, and many more are sure to come. We have seen that forgiveness isn't completely linear. It's circular and it's continuous. Yet, we have also seen there *is* a linear aspect to it. There are proven principles. There is a clear path.

I did not, and do not, ever want to become the malignant person unforgiveness will inevitably warp me into. I doubt any of us wants that.

The Third Journey: Personalizing Forgiveness

I used to live in Minnesota, where, because of the winters and the humidity and the overall wetness there, we had rust kits for our cars. We had to watch for the slightest signs of rust, always being at the ready to employ our trusty rust kits. If we didn't, it was a certainty that one day we'd discover the bottoms of our cars eaten away by rust. That is such a picture of what unforgiveness, over time, does to our souls.

So, in our attempt to live well in our two worlds, we can commit to staying alert and working hard to follow heaven's command to forgive those who have hurt us. There is a tension, yes. But we know the principles of the kingdom of heaven are right, and they are good for us. Some days will go better than others. Sometimes we will be able to forgive, and it will begin to feel as if the hurt is behind us. But then, in another moment, we will be plunged back into the dark pit of unforgiveness and anger. That is simply the nature of life in this world.

However, if we apply ourselves to the task, we can hang on to the hope that one day we can better live out our humanity, flawed as it may be, and the truth of our second citizenship will soak deeper into our souls. From this we can slowly be transformed into wounded healers, helping ourselves and others better navigate the quest for forgiveness. We will see that what is true of our second citizenship can be true here.

If we don't give up, if we tenaciously believe that what God says is true, it will change us from the inside out. The principles of forgiveness can become the change agents of our souls. We will have to stay at it. We will have to go easy on ourselves and others. But when we put heaven's principles into play, we can look at someone we once resented and begin to sense something new. We can aim to do what Irish folk singer Luka Bloom aches to accomplish in his song "Forgiveness": "Let all the hatred leave these shores now, never to return."[26]

If that sentiment sounds too lofty or too challenging an objective right now, then let us recognize that, practically speaking, our physical, emotional, and spiritual health are on the line. Let us choose not to live one more day without at least taking a step toward the process of banishing the bitterness, resentment, and hate that flow from the places of our unforgiveness.

In the next several pages, I have provided some practical ways to personalize forgiveness using prayers, poems, song, and areas for you to journal any thoughts and feelings that may arise. In my own experience, I have found that when I take time to write it down, I can turn to the pages in the future whenever I feel myself being sucked back into the vortex of unforgiveness. If you prayerfully meditate on the verses, write down your thoughts, name names, and take the time and effort to pinpoint the issues in your journey toward forgiveness, I believe it can make a demonstrable difference in your life, beginning right now.

Another practice that has helped me in my own journey, in order for me to digest what the Bible is saying about forgiveness, is crawling and limping my way through the passages and prayers by inserting my name and by pausing to reflect on how whatever I am reading is true in my own life. Whether it is David or someone else, I make their words my words, their prayers my own. It's the way I have been able to find healing, and I share that in hopes it may aid you, too.

Personalizing: Embracing Forgiveness

Reflect:

Here is a place for you to identify areas in your life where you would benefit from embracing forgiveness. Can you think of any people whom you may have mistreated or wronged? Are there any accidents or unintended events that occurred for which you may have been responsible, leaving deep scars? Where are you in the process of forgiving yourself? Be as specific as you can, journaling questions, feelings, thoughts. Are there any specific places where you have experienced victory and encouragement with forgiveness?

Pray:

Prayer is such a helpful way to apply many of the principles we've been talking about. Each of us has our own special way of communicating with God. Even so, I'd like to share with you some prayers and thoughts that have helped me greatly. If you can, try to make these pleas your own.

Psalm 51

Psalm 51 captures David's heart-wrenching journey to mend the brokenness he's created. In the first journey we spent a great deal of time looking at the life of King David. He was a person of contradictions, like many of us. He could be virtuous and courageous as well as manipulative and heartless. Many of us feel a kinship with him, though he lived thousands of years ago. We have hurt the ones we love and then had to live with the consequences. Psalm 51 was the first psalm David would pen about his relationship with another man's wife. It's a raw, gritty account of a person finally coming to grips with the awful extent of his actions. As you read this confession, this is one of those Scriptures where it can be so helpful spiritually to insert your name for his.

> *Have mercy on me, _____, O God, because of your unfailing love. Because of your great compassion, blot out the stain of my sins:_____.*
> *Wash me clean from my guilt. Purify me from my sin. For I recognize my rebellion; it haunts me day and night. Against you, and you alone, have I sinned; I have done what is evil in your sight. You will be proved right in what you say, and your judgment against me is just. For I was born a sinner—yes, from the moment my mother conceived me. But you desire honesty from the womb, teaching me wisdom even there. Purify me, _____, from my sins, and I will be clean; wash me, and I will be whiter than snow. Oh, give me back my joy again; you have broken me—now let me rejoice. [Take a moment and let this soak in. You can have joy again.] Don't keep looking at my sins. Remove the stain of my guilt. Create in me a clean heart, O God. Renew a loyal spirit within me. Do not banish me from your presence, and don't take your Holy Spirit from me, _____. Restore to me, _____, the joy of your salvation, and make me willing to obey you. Then I will teach your ways to rebels, and they will return to you. Forgive me for shedding blood [or whatever your sin or mistake may be], O God who saves; then I, _____, will joyfully sing of your forgiveness. Unseal my lips, O Lord, that my mouth may praise you. You do not desire a sacrifice or I would offer one. You do not want a burnt offering. The sacrifice you desire is a broken spirit. You will not reject a broken and repentant heart, O God.*
>
> —Psalm 51:1-17 (NLT)

Prayers for Forgiveness

As you can see, David pours out his emotions to God. He holds
nothing back. Don't be afraid to do the same. Psalms, the longest
book in the Bible, reveals the longings and prayers of the lonely,
depressed, angry, bitter, dispirited, as well as the joyful and
thankful. Reading a psalm a day can help us realize just how
genuine and real we can be with God. As we come face to face
with our most gut-wrenching regrets, we can begin to mend our
brokenness. I've included some prayers that seem to capture the
beautiful reality of our forgiven-ness.

A Cry from the Heart: I recommend praying this first short,
simple prayer whenever you feel discouraged about your ability
to forgive yourself:

> *Father, my heart cries out with sorrow and regret for the
> sin I've committed. How can I possibly forgive myself for
> such a deed? I know I've hurt You, because You love me
> so. I try and try to do what is right, but I just mess up
> time after time. Please forgive me and help me to forgive
> myself. In Jesus' name, Amen.*[27]

A Plea for Cleansing: This beautiful old prayer, created by
A. W. Tozer, may reflect the longing of your heart as you seek to
receive forgiveness:

> *O Lord, I have heard a good word inviting me to look away
> to Thee and be satisfied. My heart longs to respond, but
> sin has clouded my vision till I see Thee but dimly. Be
> pleased to cleanse me in Thine own precious blood, and
> make me inwardly pure, so that I may with unveiled eyes
> gaze upon Thee all the days of my earthly pilgrimage.
> Then shall I be prepared to behold Thee in full splendor*

in the day when Thou shalt appear to be glorified in Thy
saints and admired in all them that believe. Amen.[28]

Sing/Recite:

A song can communicate emotions that spoken words may not fully get across. Even though the lyrics to "Amazing Grace" may be very familiar, try reading them slowly and carefully, without being distracted from their profundity because of their familiarity.

As you may recall, the author of "Amazing Grace" was John Newton, who called himself a "wretch" who was lost and blind, having lived the heinous life of a slave-trading ship's captain. On one of his journeys to capture more slaves in West Africa during the 18th century, a fierce storm erupted, and Newton was overcome by the fear of a shipwreck, realizing for the first time that only by God's grace could he be spared. Shortly thereafter, he began reading *The Imitation of Christ* by Thomas à Kempis. This book became a key ingredient in leading him to place his faith in Christ as his Savior. Leaving his wicked way of life behind, Newton entered the ministry full-time in England and never stopped proclaiming God's grace. He had received forgiveness and would never be the same. "Amazing Grace" is the story of his life and the story of ours:

Amazing Grace—how sweet the sound—
that saved a wretch like me!
I once was lost but now am found,
was blind but now I see.
'Twas grace that taught my heart to fear,
and grace my fears relieved;
How precious did that grace appear
the hour I first believed!
Through many dangers, toils and snares,
I have already come;

'Tis grace has brought me safe thus far,
and grace will lead me home.
The Lord has promised good to me;
His word my hope secures;
He will my shield and portion be
as long as life endures.[29]

Receive:

The Ultimate Gift, Salvation

We have been talking about this gift of forgiveness and, at this point, if you haven't ever accepted God's forgiveness and made a decision to follow Jesus, maybe this prayer would be an inspiration for you. Again, prayer is simply talking to God as we would to a friend. No need for high and holy language. Prayer is the way we express our desire to know God and to receive his forgiveness. If you are ready to pray such a prayer, perhaps this one will be of help:

Dear God, I know that I have really messed up my life by wrong, hurtful ways of thinking and behaving. I finally realize that I need to receive you, Jesus, as my Lord and Savior. Thank you for dying on the cross for my sins. Thank you for forgiving me fully and completely. I just cannot believe you would love me enough to do that. Please, take up residence in my life and make me the kind of person you want me to be. In Jesus' name, Amen.

If you prayed this prayer in faith, Jesus now lives in your heart and spirit. I know it is all new and maybe a little strange. But trust me, you are beginning the greatest adventure of your life. As a new believer, you will benefit from finding a healthy church with loving believers who can nurture, guide, and try to answer your questions. Also, try to find a version of the Bible that may be easier to understand and appreciate, like the *New Living Translation*, the *New International Version* (the translation I've used most in this book), or *The Message*. If you have questions, please feel free to contact me via my website: www.BarbaraFrancis.com.

Help Along the Journey

I've suggested quite a few prayers and songs in this section. Maybe you'd like to add some of your own favorites here:

Personalizing: Extending Forgiveness

Reflect:

Here's another opportunity to journal. This time try to put in writing incidences or people in your life whom you find impossible to forgive. I know this is delicate ground. The wounds may be too deep, the violations too unspeakable. I wouldn't suggest writing these down if I hadn't done so myself and found it immeasurably helpful. There will be a few of you who, like me, are finding a growing measure of victory in the forgiveness realm. Record the names of people with whom you're making progress, as well. Take your time. This is a needed, albeit difficult, exercise to complete. These are the very people and memories we need, by God's grace, to extend forgiveness to:

Pray:

We've been taking an arduous and grueling path through a very difficult topic—describing areas in your life where you struggle most with forgiving. You have probably recalled some of the painful emotions associated with the people and events you have been thinking and writing about. Dealing with the ferocity of emotions can be overwhelming. (In fact, in some instances, you may want to seek out a friend or even a competent professional therapist to see if it'd be advisable to get some extra help and counseling.) Below is a collection of prayers and meditations that can help you deal with the strong feelings and emotions that are typically part of this process.

A Prayer About Rage

This first prayer, written by Christian spirituality expert Richard Foster, grew out of a request from a woman who, through much counseling, had made significant progress in dealing with her childhood sexual abuse. She was hoping for a prayer to help her deal with the lingering rage. However, *your* battlefield may be something quite unlike childhood abuse, so, again, I invite you to bring your personal struggle to let go and forgive into this moving prayer:

I. Acknowledgement

Dear God, I come to you with an overwhelming anger, a bursting rage. This rage is like a cancer shut up in my bones, eating away at my soul. Today, O God, I acknowledge this rage; I do not suppress it, or hide it. Thank you, Lord, thank you, for accepting me rage and all.

II. Expression

O God, I feel a burning rage within, a fire gone wild. Burning, always burning. God, I hate what was done to me. It was so evil. So wrong. Why this evil? Why this degradation? Why? Why? Why? My rage, O God, is the only power I have against this vicious world. That's why I cannot let it go. Please God, don't ask me to let it go.

III. Turning

God, I cannot separate my hatred for what was done from the person who did it. I despise the deed. I loathe the person who did the deed. My rage is my only revenge. But, God, my rage destroys me too. I feel this seething anger searing my own soul. O Lord, my God, deliver me from the evil I would do to myself.

IV. Forgiving

I refuse to allow this evil to control me anymore. I will not be held in bondage to my hate any longer. But, the strength to love is not in me. I must wait for your enabling. Now, in your great power, and with a trembling heart, I speak your word of forgiveness.[30]

A Personal Prayer for Forgiveness

This is a bold prayer to forgive the ones who have come against you, leaving you wounded. I know these words will not be easy to say as you picture in your mind those who have wronged you. I wrote this prayer for myself as I sought to put into practice the very exercises I am encouraging you to engage in.

When you pray this prayer, I strongly encourage you to personalize it with your own story. Pray this prayer often as you walk the painful, difficult road toward extending forgiveness:

Lord Jesus, you know how hurt I am. My heart is broken by betrayal, false accusations, cruel comments, or _____. I desperately want your help to forgive _____. Your word is clear: "Forgive as the Lord forgave you" (Colossians 3:13). Jesus modeled it while hanging on a cross so I, yes I, could be forgiven: "Father, forgive them" (Luke 23:34). The cry of my heart and the commitment of my life are to be pure inside and out. Unforgiveness sullies my soul and robs me of your peace.

I cannot control how _____ will continue to respond to me. I will no longer wait for them to change. I will no longer judge them in my heart and speak about their wrongs against me to others. Please, allow no root of bitterness to bud in my heart (Hebrews 12:14-15). Ultimately, that vicious vine would choke the very life out of me. I don't want to just "get through" this hurt, but to flourish and grow because authentic forgiveness has been extended. By your grace and strength I will lean into your forgiveness of _____. I choose now to fully forgive them. And, when their faces pop into my mind or I am reminded of ways they have _____ me, I will not only forgive them, but also bless them, just as Jesus commanded: "Bless those who curse you, and pray for those who mistreat you" (Luke 6:28). Help me to recall all the positive ways you have used these people in my life. I will pray that _____ will experience personal spiritual revival. I will pray blessings into all aspects of their lives.

I accept the reality that our relationship may never be what it was before the event, and yet I ask that you would restore and heal wherever possible. Thank you for revealing the truth that I can still experience the full personal benefits of forgiveness even if _____ never own their part in hurting me so terribly.

In Jesus' name, Amen.

Sing/Recite:

This classic song by Don Henley is raw with emotion. Its lack of punctuation makes it all the more so. Yet in spite of the obvious pain expressed in it, it contains the undeniable truth that forgiveness is the only way to recovery.

Im learning to live without you now
But I miss you baby
And the more I know the less I understand
All the things I thought Id figured out
I have to learn again
Ive been trying to get down
To the heart of the matter
But everything changes
And my friends seem to scatter
But I think its about forgiveness
Forgiveness
Even if even if you don't love me anymore
There are people in your life whove come and gone
They let you down you know they hurt your pride
You better put it all behind you baby life goes on
You keep carrying that anger itll eat you up inside baby
Ive been trying to get down
To the heart of the matter
But my will gets weak
And my thoughts seem to scatter
But I think its about forgiveness
Forgiveness
Even if even if you dont love me anymore[31]

Receive:

Take time to add your own favorite prayers, poetry, or song lyrics that have helped you extend forgiveness:

Hopeful Words from God

In this final section I want to simply write out verses from the Bible to soothe and comfort as you learn to forgive yourself and others. These words lend perspective while you heal, and they offer hope for better days ahead.

The Bible contains promises of God's presence, comfort, and love no matter our mood. I hope you'll return again and again to read these healing words. Make the promises real for your life and circumstances. But first, let's consider a clarifying prayer for reflection. Once our battle is clear, then we can freely receive God's whispers of love and courage.

> *Thank you that You have me in the place You want me just now...that even if I got here through wrong choices or indifference or even rebellion, yet You knew my mistakes and sins before I ever existed, and You worked them into Your plan to draw me to Yourself, to mold and bless me, and to bless others through me. Thank You that, even if I'm here through the ill-will or poor judgment of other people, all is well; for in Your sovereign wisdom You are at work to bring about good results from all those past decisions, those past events beyond my control—good results both for me and for others. Amen.*[32]

Find rest, O my soul, in God alone; my hope comes from him. He alone is my rock and my salvation; he is my fortress, I will not be shaken. My salvation and my honor depend on God; he is my mighty rock, my refuge. Trust in him at all times, O people; pour out your hearts to him, for God is our refuge.

—Psalm 62:5-8

I lift up my eyes to the hills—where does my help come from? My help comes from the Lord, the Maker of heaven and earth. He will not let your foot slip—he who watches over you will not slumber; indeed, he who watches over Israel will neither slumber nor sleep.

—*Psalm 121:1-4*

Hurry with your answer, God! I'm nearly at the end of my rope. Don't turn away; don't ignore me! That would be certain death. If you wake me each morning with the sound of your loving voice, I'll go to sleep each night trusting in you. Point out the road I must travel; I'm all ears, all eyes before you. Save me from my enemies, God—you're my only hope! Teach me how to live to please you, because you're my God. Lead me by your blessed Spirit into cleared and level pastureland.

—*Psalm 143:7-10 (TM)*

Seek the Lord while he's here to be found, pray to him while he's close at hand. Let the wicked abandon their way of life and the evil their way of thinking. Let them come back to God, who is merciful, come back to our God, who is lavish with forgiveness.

—*Isaiah 55:6-7 (TM)*

For I know the plans I have for you, says the Lord. They are plans for good and not for evil, to give you a future and a hope.

—*Jeremiah 29:11 (TLB)*

(Jesus speaking) You're blessed when you're at the end of your rope. With less of you there is more of God and his rule. You're blessed when you feel you've lost what is most dear to you. Only then can you be embraced by the One most dear to you. You're blessed when you're content with just who you are—no more, no less. That's the moment you find yourselves proud owners of everything that can't be bought. You're blessed when you've worked up a good appetite for God. He's food and drink in the best meal you'll ever eat. You're blessed when you care. At the moment of being 'care-full,' you find yourselves cared for. You're blessed when you get your inside world—your mind and heart—

put right. Then you can see God in the outside world. You're blessed when you can show people how to cooperate instead of compete or fight. That's when you discover who you really are, and your place in God's family. You're blessed when your commitment to God provokes persecution. The persecution drives you even deeper into God's kingdom.

—Matthew 5:3-10 (TM)

Don't fret or worry. Instead of worrying, pray. Let petitions and praises shape your worries into prayers, letting God know your concerns. Before you know it, a sense of God's wholeness, everything coming together for good, will come and settle you down. It's wonderful what happens when Christ displaces worry at the center of your life.

—Philippians 4:6-7 (TM)

And we know that in all things God works for the good for those who love him, who have been called according to his purpose.

—Romans 8:28

For I am convinced that neither death nor life, neither angels nor demons, neither the present nor the future, nor any powers, neither height nor depth, nor anything else in all creation, will be able to separate us from the love of God that is in Christ Jesus our Lord.

—Romans 8:38-39

But the Lord is faithful, and he will strengthen and protect you from the evil one.... May the Lord direct your hearts into God's love and Christ's perseverance.

—2 Thessalonians 3:3, 5

Come near to God and he will come near to you.

—James 4:8

Let him have all your worries and cares, for he is always thinking about you and watching everything that concerns you.... After you have suffered a little while, our God, who is full of kindness through Christ, will give you his eternal glory. He personally will come and pick you up, and set you firmly in place, and make you stronger than ever.

—*1 Peter 5:7, 10-11 (TLB)*

The Father's love does not force itself on the beloved. Although he wants to heal us of all our inner darkness, we are still free to make our own choice to stay in the darkness or to step into the light of God's love. God is there. God's light is there. God's forgiveness is there, always ready to give and forgive.[33]

—Henri Nouwen

Notes

Notes

Notes

Notes

Notes

Notes

Endnotes

Introduction:

[1] St. John of the Ladder, as quoted in *Reaching Out* by Henri J. M. Nouwen, Image Books, A Division of Doubleday & Company, Garden City, NY, 1986, p. 15.

[2] Lewis Smedes, *Forgive and Forget: Healing the Hurts We Don't Deserve*, Harper One, A Division of Harper Collins Publishers, New York, NY, 1984, p. xvi.

[3] Prayer of St. Ignatius of Loyola (1491-1556), http://www.sacredspace.ie.

The First Journey:

[4] Dag Hammarskjold, *Markings*, Ballantine Books, A Division of Random House, Inc., New York, NY, 1983, p. 105.

[5] Vernon Grounds, as quoted in *Rebuilding Your Broken World* by Gordon McDonald, Oliver Nelson, A Division of Thomas Nelson Publishers, Nashville, TN, 1988, p. xi.

[6] Mason Jennings, "Forgiveness," www.masonjennings.com/music.

[7] Annie Dillard, *The Writing Life*, HarperCollins, New York, NY, 1989, p. 32.

[8] Bono, "It's 2009. Do You Know Where Your Soul Is?" *The New York Times*, New York, NY, April 19, 2009, Op-Ed Section, p. WK11 of the New York edition.

[9]Elie Wiesel, "A Prayer for the Days of Awe," *The New York Times*, New York, NY, Oct. 2, 1997, Op-Ed, A Section, p. 19 of the New York edition.

[10]Robert Robertson, "Come Thou Fount of Every Blessing," as quoted in *Amazing Grace: 366 Hymn Stories for Personal Devotion* by Kenneth W. Osbeck, Kregel Publications, Grand Rapids, MI, 1990, p. 343.

[11]*Oxford American Dictionary*, Heald Colleges Edition, Avon Books, An Imprint of Harper Collins Publishers, New York, NY, 1980, p. 347.

The Second Journey:

[12]Martin Luther King, Jr., as quoted in *Reflections on the Word* by Ken Gire, Chariot Victor Publishing, Colorado Springs, CO, 1998, p. 78.

[13]Margaret Thatcher, BBC, http://news.bbc.co.uk/onthisday/hi/dates/stories/november/8/newsid_2515000/2515113.stm.

[14]Gordon Wilson, Spirit of Enniskillen Trust, www.soetrust.co.uk/index.php?id=5.

[15]Jonathan Bardon, as quoted in "Heroes—Gordon and Joan Wilson," Brits at their Best, www.britsattheirbest.com/001668.php.

[16]Henri J. M. Nouwen, *The Only Necessary Thing*, compiled and edited by Wendy Wilson Greer, The Crossroad Publishing Company, New York, NY, 1999, p. 150.

[17]Anne Lamott, *Traveling Mercies*, Anchor Books, A Division of Random House, Inc., New York, NY, 2000, p. 134.

[18]*Oxford American Dictionary*, Heald Colleges Edition, Avon Books, An Imprint of Harper Collins Publishers, New York, NY, 1980, p. 173.

[19]Max Lucado, *No Wonder They Call Him the Savior*, Multnomah Press, Sisters, OR, 1986, pp. 24-25.

[20]Saint Augustine, "Augustine of Hippo," Wikiquote, http://en.wikiquote.org/wiki/Augustine_of_Hippo.

[21]Richard J. Foster, *Prayer: Finding the Heart's True Home,* Harper San Francisco, A Division of Harper Collins Publishers, New York, NY, 1992, p. 188.

[22]Henri J. M. Nouwen, *The Only Necessary Thing,* compiled and edited by Wendy Wilson Greer, Crossroad Publishing, New York, NY, 1999, p. 155.

[23]Charles Stanley, as quoted in *The Spirit of Revival Magazine,* a publication of LifeAction Ministries, August 1993, p. 13.

[24]Lewis Smedes, *Forgive and Forget: Healing the Hurts We Don't Deserve,* Harper One, A Division of Harper Collins Publishers, New York, NY, 1984, p. 54.

The Third Journey:

[25]Laurence Sterne, as quoted in *Treasury of Thought* by Maturin Murray Ballou, Houghton, Mifflin and Company, Boston, MA, 1882, p. 183.

[26]Luka Bloom, "Forgiveness," www.lukabloom.comsaltyheaven_l.php#11

[27]Anita Corrine Donihue, *When I'm on My Knees,* Barbour Publishers, Uhrichsville, OH, 1997, p. 55.

[28]A. W. Tozer, *The Pursuit of God,* Tyndale House Publishers, Wheaton, IL, 1982, p. 98.

[29]John Newton, "Amazing Grace," as quoted in *Amazing Grace: 366 Hymn Stories for Personal Devotion* by Kenneth W. Osbeck, Kregel Publications, Grand Rapids, MI, 1990, p. 170.

[30]Richard J. Foster, *Prayers from the Heart,* Harper San Francisco, A Division of Harper Collins Publishers, New York, NY, 1992, pp. 14-17.

[31]Don Henley, "The Heart of the Matter," http://www.lyricsfreak.com.

[32]Ruth Myers, *31 Days of Praise,* Multnomah Publishers, Inc., Sisters, OR, 1994, p. 76.

[33]Henri J. M. Nouwen, source unknown.

About the Author

It may seem odd that Barbara Francis has written a book on forgiveness—because it's been a struggle for her to receive forgiveness personally and to give it to others. Even when she became a follower of Christ in college, forgiveness remained elusive. And, frankly, it still is. Perfection is beyond slippery when it comes to the topic of forgiveness. But perfection isn't Barbara's goal—growth is.

Grace & Guts: What It Takes to Forgive tracks her growth process in an honest and personal way. And the good news is that growth can happen for all who make the hard choice to be passionately candid with their struggle, *whatever* it may be, to bring it boldly to God in prayer, and to ask for his help in doing what they cannot do themselves. God knows life is messy. Barbara knows it, too, and takes this realistic approach to all areas of life. Thanks to a refreshing authenticity, Barbara is a popular, sought-after communicator. Her conversational and compelling style, relevant teaching of God's word, and down-to-earth principles for resolution speak hope to audiences and readers of all ages in a variety of countries. People connect. People are helped.

Barbara has been married and in ministry for quite some time, has two beloved grown children, and is "Nana" to two superb grandchildren.

Check out Barbara's web site at www.BarbaraFrancis.com and her new blog site at www.graceandguts.net.